MAULANA ABUL KALAM AZAD AND APJ ABDUL KALAM

Exemplary Legends for All Times

MAULANA ABUL KALAM AZAD AND APJ ABDUL KALAM
Exemplary Legends for All Times

Khwaja Abdul Muntaqim

KALPAZ

ISBN: 978-93-5128-182-5

Price: ₹ 580

First Published, 2016

Published by

Kalpaz Publications
C-30, Satyawati Nagar,
Delhi – 110052
E-mail: kalpaz@hotmail.com
Ph.: 9212142040

Printed at: G. Print Process, Delhi

Cataloging in Publication Data—DK

Courtesy: D.K. Agencies (P) Ltd. <docinfo@dkagencies.com>

Muntaqim, Khwaja A. (Khwaja Abdul), author.

Maulana Abul Kalam Azad and APJ Abdul Kalam : exemplary legends for all times / Khwaja Abdul Muntaqim.

pages cm

ISBN 9789351281825

1. Āzād, Abūlkalām, 1888-1958. 2. Statesmen—India—Biography. 3. Scholars—India—Biography. 4. Abul Kalam, A. P. J. (Avul Pakir Jainulabdeen), 1931-2015. 5. Presidents—India—Biography. 6. Scientists—India—Biography. I. Title.

DS481.A9M86 2016 DDC 954.035092 23

Contents

Preface

The title of the book "*Maulana Abul Kalam Azad and APJ Abdul Kalam...Exemplary Legends for All Times*" is self-explanatory. It is an objective assessment of the contribution of these two great personalities to the country and the nation. We celebrate our Independence day on August, 15 every year. It is our duty to remember our freedom fighters and strugglers like Mahatma Gandhi, Pandit Jawahar Lal Nehru, Sardar Patel, Maulana Abul Kalam Azad, Bal Ganga Dhar Tilak, Sarojini Naidu, Lala Lajpat Rai, Acharya J B Kripalani, Lal Bahadur Shastri, Morarji Desai, and many other such great personalities including many an unsung hero as also martyrs like Shaheed Bhagat Singh, Chandra Shekhar Azad, Ashfaqullah Khan and many others on this auspicious day not merely for paying tribute to them but to perpetuate their memory so that the younger generation may not forget and ignore them.

Narendra Modi, Chief Minister of Gujarat (as he then was, presently the Prime Minister of India) writing in his blog on the occasion of the 125th birth anniversaries of Maulana Abul Kalam Azad and Acharya J B Kripalani, had expressed the view "It is with deep anguish that I see how some of our friends have reduced stalwarts of the freedom struggle to mere partisan political leaders. There can be no greater disservice to our history than viewing these stalwarts through the narrow prism of political partisanship."

(Gandhinagar (Gujarat), Nov.11 (ANI) Gujarat)

Maulana Abul Kalam Azad, one of the greatest Indian freedom strugglers and fighters, secular to the marrow of his bones, an icon of true secularism and religious neutrality, a distinguished and renowned scholar and poet, a man of luminous intelligence and mighty intellect, a prolific writer, a revolutionary journalist, a brilliant debater and speaker, a person with scientific temperament, a great statesman, a man of action and above all a person with great vision and liberal outlook as also the architect of Modern Indian Education System, would be remembered throughout for his political achievements and the sacrifices he made for the country in a very difficult and extremely adverse situation as also stiff opposition from his own community (pre-partition Muslims).

As regards APJ Abdul Kalam, a great scientist, popularly known as missile man, a gentleman of the first order, recognised and loved as a national hero for his valuable contribution in the field of space research would be remembered for his technical contribution to the country and as a symbol and practical example of India really being a secular country –a country in which son of a Muslim fisherman can get an opportunity to receive best education and become head of state of the biggest democracy of the world.

Let the nation salute both of them for centuries and centuries to come.

Hazaron saal Nargis apni benoori pe roti hai
bari mushkil se hota(e) hai(n) chaman mein didawar paida

For a thousand years the Narcissus has been lamenting its blindness; With great difficulty the one(s) with true vision is (are) born.

The book contains 13 chapters captioned Biography of Maulana Abul Kalam Azad, Maulana Azad's Strong Opposition to the Partition of India, Views of Eminent National and

International Figures about Maulana Azad, Maulana's Major Works and Quotable Quotes, Maulana's Views on Partition (in the form of a monologue, that is, a presumptive soliloquy), Maulana's Views on Hindu Muslim Unity, Constitutional Mandate for Religious Harmony and National Integration, Had Maulana been alive to watch the present day situation of Muslims live and fix the responsibility, Maulana Azad as a Champion of Human Rights, Maulana Azad an exceptionally honest and corruption free personality, Author's Tribute to A.P.J. Abdul Kalam and his appreciative sermons, Biography of A.P.J. Abdul Kalam and Maulana Abul Kalam Azad and APJ Abdul Kalam -A note of commendation.

The book is free from any controversial statement, description, criticism or condemnation *qua* any individual, political party, group of people or religion/faith. I believe that it is a unique academic venture to be appreciated by readers with non-jaundiced eyes.

—Khwaja Abul Muntaqim

H-3, Dharma Apartments,
2-I.P. Extn., Delhi-110092
E-mail: amkhwaja2007@yahoo.co.in

Epitome

India, that is Bharat, as so named in Article 1 of the Indian Constitution, won freedom on August 15, 1947 but Maulana Abul Kalam Azad lost the political battle as Partition hurt him badly and shattered his dream of an unified free India where Hindus and Muslims could co-exist and prosper together as good people, good citizens and as equal partners. The following speech of Maulana Azad delivered at Jama Masjid (Grand Mosque), Delhi, October 23, 1947 bears testimony to it:

"My brethren,

You know what has brought me here today. This congregation at Shahjehan's historic mosque is not an unfamiliar sight for me. Here, I have addressed you on several previous occasions. Since then we have seen many ups and downs. At that time, instead of weariness, your faces reflected serenity, and your hearts, instead of misgivings, exuded confidence. The uneasiness on your faces and the desolation in your hearts that I see today, reminds me of the events of the past few years.

Do you remember? I hailed you, you cut off my tongue; I picked my pen, you severed my hand; I wanted to move forward, you broke off my legs; I tried to run, and you injured my back. When the bitter political games of the last seven years were at their peak, I tried to wake you up at every danger signal. You not only ignored my call but revived all the past traditions of neglect and denial. As a result the same perils surround you today, whose onset had previously diverted you from the righteous path.

Today, mine is no more than an inert existence or a forlorn cry; I am an orphan in my own motherland. This does not mean that I feel trapped in the original choice that had made for myself, nor do I feel that there is no room left for my *ashiana* (nest). What it means is that my cloak is weary of your impudent grabbing hands. My sensitivities are injured, my heart is heavy. Think for one moment. What course did you adopt? Where have you reached, and where do you stand now? Haven't your senses become torpid? Aren't you living in a constant state of fear? This fear is your own creation, a fruit of your own deeds.

It was not long ago when I warned you that the two-nation theory was death-knell to a meaningful, dignified life; forsake it. I told you that the pillars upon which you were leaning would inevitably crumble. To all this you turned a deaf ear. You did not realise that, my brothers! I have always attempted to keep politics apart from personalities, thus avoiding those thorny valleys. That is why some of my messages are often couched in allusions. The partition of India was a fundamental mistake. The manner in which religious differences were incited, inevitably, led to the devastation that we have seen with our own eyes. Unfortunately, we are still seeing it at some places.

There is no use recounting the events of the past seven years, nor will it serve any good. Yet, it must be stated that the debacle of Indian Muslims is the result of the colossal blunders committed by the Muslim League's misguided leadership. These consequences, however, were no surprise to me; I had anticipated them from the very start.

Now that Indian politics has taken a new direction, there is no place in it for the Muslim League. Now the question is whether or not we are capable of constructive thinking. For this, I have invited the Muslim leaders of India to Delhi, during the second week of November.

The gloom cast upon your lives is momentary; I assure you we can be beaten by none save our own selves! I have always said, and I repeat it again today; eschew your indecisiveness, your mistrust, and stop your misdeeds. This unique triple-edged weapon is more lethal than the two-edged iron sword which inflicts fatal wounds, which I have heard of !

Just think about the life of escapism that you have opted for, in the sacred name of Hejrat (migration). Get into the habit of exercising your own brains, and strengthening your own hearts. If you do so, only then will you realise how immature your decisions were.

Where are you going and why? Raise your eyes. The minarets of Jama Masjid want to ask you a question. Where have you lost the glorious pages from your chronicles? Was it only yesterday that on the banks of the Jamuna, your caravans performed *wuzu* (ablution)? Today, you are afraid of living here! Remember, Delhi has been nurtured with your blood. Brothers! Create a basic change in yourselves. Today, your fear is misplaced as your jubilation was yesterday.

The words coward and frenzy cannot be spoken in the same breath as the word Muslim. A true Muslim can be swayed neither by avarice nor apprehension. Don't get scared because a few faces have disappeared. The only reason they had herded you in a single fold was to facilitate their own flight. Today, if they have jerked their hand free from yours, what does it matter? Make sure that they have not run away with your hearts. If your hearts are still in the right place, make them the abode of God. Some thirteen hundred years ago, through an Arab ummi (unlettered) prophet Muhammad (S), God proclaimed, "Those who place their faith in God and are firm in their belief, no fear for them nor any sorrow." Winds blow in and blow out: tempests may gather but all this is short-lived. The period of trial is about to end. Change yourselves as if you had never been in such an abject condition.

I am not used to altercation. Faced with your general indifference, however, I will repeat that the third force has departed, and along with it, its trappings of vanity. Whatever had to happen has happened. If your hearts have still not changed and your minds still have reservations, it is a different matter. But, if you want a change, then take your cue from history, and cast yourself in the new mould. Having completed a revolutionary phase, there still remain a few blank pages in the history of India. You can make ourselves worthy of filling those pages, provided you are willing.

Brothers! Keep up with the changes. Don't say, "We are not ready for the change." Get ready. Stars may have plummeted down but the sun is still shining. Borrow a few of its rays and sprinkle them in the dark caverns of your lives.

I do not ask you to seek certificates from the new echelons of power. I do not want you to lead a life of sycophancy as you did during the foreign rule. I want you to remind you that these bright etchings which you see all around you are relics of qafilas (caravans of the celebrities) of your forefathers. Do not forget them. Do not forsake them. Live like their worthy inheritors, and, rest assured, that if you do not wish to flee from this scene, nobody can make you flee. Come, today let us pledge that this country is ours, we belong to it and any fundamental decisions about its destiny will remain incomplete without our consent.

Today, you fear the earth's tremors; once you were virtually the earthquake itself. Today, you fear the darkness; once your existence was the epicenter of radiance. Clouds have poured dirty waters and you have hitched up your trousers. Those were none but your forefathers who not only plunged headlong into the seas, but trampled the mountains, laughed at the bolts of lightning, turned away the tornados, challenged the tempests and made them alter their course. It is a sure sign of a dying faith that those who had once grabbed the collars of emperors, are today, clutching their own throats. They have become oblivious of the existence of God as if they had never believed in Him.

Brothers! I do not have a new prescription for you. I have the same old prescription that was revealed to the greatest benefactor of mankind, the prescription of the Holy Quran: "Do not fear and do not grieve. If you possess true faith, you will gain the upper hand." The congregation is now at an end. What I had to say, I have said, briefly. Let me say once again, keep a grip on your senses. Learn to create your own surroundings, your own world. This is not a commodity that I can buy for you from the market-place. This can be bought only from the market-place of the heart, provided you can pay for it with the currency of good deeds.

May God's grace be on you!"

Had there been no partition or the process of partition and migration of population (if considered inevitable) been managed properly, the human massacre on both the sides in which more than a million people were killed, several millions displaced and many more cut off from their roots, could be avoided. Parents got separated from their children, friends lost their friends, and lovers lost their dear ones. Sometimes, it is said that the Partition of India was the cultural death of India's composite culture or, if described in present day terminology, it was the death of the then almost united civil society. It may not be absolutely true as composite culture of India survived even after partition as majority of Muslims preferred to stay in India.

Partition was not only the logical outcome of Britain's policy of 'divide and rule' but it was also an economic compulsion for the Britishers as they were not in a position to afford the cost of ruling this country because of having suffered heavy losses in Second World War. However, for the people of India and the geographers it was the geographical slaughter of the Indian dominion as its pious land was surgically divided and a new state 'Pakistan' was carved out of it. Even fauna and flora and rivers and streams were not spared. For supporters of Jinnah's two-nation theory and those demanding a separate homeland, that is, Pakistan, it was the fulfillment of their cherished desire and the recognition of their struggle to have their separate identity. For the Bangladeshis, then known as Bengalis, who were the frontline supporters of Pak movement was a deceptive dawn that proved to be the prelude to their achievement of their own country named "Bangladesh" in 1971, a prediction by Maulana Azad, proved to be a reality. For freedom fighters; it was the glorious result of their movement. For the rest of the world and the world history, it was one of the most important events of twentieth-century. For the international civil society, it was a badly managed shameful end of Britain's imperial rule in India that proved a tragic and horrible experience for the hundreds of thousands of Hindus, Sikhs and Muslims who were killed in the communal holocaust and nearly 15 million having become refugees in their homeland. Even after partition, over the past six decades India and Pakistan have been in a state of constant confrontation fighting several wars and indulging in day-to-day skirmishes.

Communal situation even before partition was not so rosy but it was not as thorny as it became after partition. None can deny that the Partition far from solving the communal problem in India, further aggravated the situation as a considerable number of Hindus, the majority community, was of the view that Indian Muslims were responsible for the partition of the country and that they betrayed them and got the country partitioned. Indian Muslims, too, played an appreciable role in freedom movement, may not be as unitedly and cohesively as their Hindu brothers did, but unfortunately the role of a class of Muslims, particularly the Muslim theologists, in India's freedom struggle has not been portrayed properly. Can anyone deny that the then Ulema of Deoband, with resoluteness and trust in God, had always been not only in the foremost rank of those who had struggled in the movement for the independence of India. Most of these gentlemen raised the banner of revolt against the English government, fought face to face with the English army and many of them passed a good part of their lives in jail.

Chapter 1

Biography of Maulana Abul Kalam Azad (1888-1958)

Maulana Abul Kalam Azad, his real name being Abul Kalam Ghulam Muhiyuddin, one of the greatest Indian freedom strugglers and fighters, secular to the marrow of his bones, an icon of true secularism and religious neutrality, a distinguished and renowned scholar and poet, a man of luminous intelligence and mighty intellect, a prolific writer, a revolutionary journalist, a brilliant debater and speaker (true to his name Abul Kalam, which literally means "an eloquent speaker"), a person with scientific temperament, a great statesman, a man of action described by certain scribes as a person of the caliber of Plato, Aristotle and Pythagoras and above all a person with great vision and liberal outlook as also the architect of Modern Indian Education System, well versed in many languages viz. Arabic, English, Urdu, Hindi, Persian and Bengali, a truly multi-cultural personality, was born on November 11, 1888 in Mecca in an orthodox religious family. His forefathers came from Herat (a city in Afghanistan). His mother was an Arab. She was the daughter of Sheikh Mohammad Zaher Watri. His father, Maulana Mohammad Khairuddin, was a Bengali Muslim gentleman of Afghan origin. He left India during Sepoy Mutiny, proceeded to Mecca, the holy city in Saudi Arabia and settled there.

He came back to Calcutta (now named as Kolkata) alongwith his family in 1890 during British rule in India. His wife died during three years of his incarceration. He was not even permitted to meet her before her death. They had no children. Dr Najma A. Heptulla, Union Minister of Minority Affairs, happens to be the grand-niece of Maulana Abul Kalam Azad.

Maulana Azad was imparted religious education to become a Maulvi (a clergyman in holy Islamic order) who may become an Imam (one who leads the prayer) or Mufti (a juri consult who notifies the decisions of the Muslim Law, in or representing, cases submitted to him or an expounder of Muslim Law) subsequently. He was taught Arabic and Persian first to get himself acquainted with Muslim Theology and jurisprudence and then Philosophy, Geometry, Mathematics and Algebra. It was through self-study that he also learnt English, world history, and political science so that he may keep pace with the changing world and acquire latest knowledge about modern world and changing global socio-political scenario.The following extract from the short biography of Maulana Azad published by Maulana Abul Kalam Azad Institute of Asian Studies (an Autonomous Body under the Ministry of Culture, Govt. of India), Kolkata, is the brief authentic version of the academic, social and political life of Maulana Azad.

"In 1912, Maulana Abul Kalam Azad started a weekly journal in Urdu called Al-Hilal to increase the revolutionary recruits amongst the Muslims. Al-Hilal played an important role in forging Hindu-Muslim unity after the bad blood created between the two communities in the aftermath of Morley-Minto reforms. Al-Hilal became a revolutionary mouthpiece ventilating extremist views. 'The government regarded Al- Hilal as propagator of secessionist views and banned it in 1914. Maulana Abul Kalam Azad then started another weekly called Al-Balagh with the same mission of propagating Indian nationalism and revolutionary ideas based on Hindu-Muslim unity. In 1916, the government banned this paper, too, and expelled Maulana Abul Kalam Azad from Calcutta and interned him at Ranchi from where he was released after the First World War in 1920.

After his release, Azad roused the Muslim community through the Khilafat Movement. The aim of the movement was to re-instate the Khalifa as the head of British captured Turkey. Maulana Abul Kalam Azad supported Non-Cooperation Movement started by Gandhiji and entered Indian National Congress in 1920. He was elected as the president of the special session of the Congress in Delhi (1923). Maulana Azad was again arrested in 1930 for violation of the salt laws as part of Gandhiji's Salt Satyagraha. He was put in Meerut jail for a year and a half. Maulana Abul Kalam Azad became the president of Congress in 1940 (Ramgarh) and remained in the post till 1946. (Author's note: After the rejection of the May 16 Plan in July 1946, Maulana Azad, who, according to some political analysts, had became a non-entity on the Indian political scene. May 16, 1946 Plan *inter alia* contained the following recommendations:

The Constitution taking the following basic form:

(1) There should be a Union of India, embracing both British India and the States which should deal with the following subjects: Foreign Affairs, Defence, and Communications; and should have the powers necessary to raise the finances required for the above subjects.

(2) The Union should have an Executive and a Legislature constituted from British Indian and States' representatives. Any question raising a major communal issue in the Legislature should require for its decision a majority of the representatives present and voting of each of the two major communities as well as a majority of all members present and voting.

(3) All subjects other than the Union subjects and all residuary powers should vest in the Provinces.

(4) The States will retain all subjects and powers other than those ceded to the Union.

(5) Provinces should be free to form groups with Executives and Legislatures, and each group could determine the Provincial subjects to be taken in common.

(6) The Constitutions of the Union and of the groups should contain a provision whereby any Province could by majority vote of its Legislative Assembly could call for a reconsideration of the terms of the Constitution after an initial period of ten years and at ten-yearly intervals thereafter.

Maulana Abul Kalam Azad served as the Minister of Education (the first education minister in independent India) in Pandit Jawaharlal Nehru's cabinet from 1947 to 1958. He died of a stroke on February 22, 1958. For his invaluable contribution to the nation, Maulana Abul Kalam Azad was posthumously awarded India's highest civilian honour, Bharat Ratna in 1992."

Maulana Azad never played in the hands of communalists. After Independence, some of those supporting Muslim League started changing their colours. They, that is, old supporters of Muslim League who had not migrated to Pakistan and who called him a 'show boy' started calling him Imamul-Hind but Maulana did not respond to their call because he did not believe in partisan politics, be it in pre-Independence or post-Independence India. He never compromised on his basic political principles and values.

CHAPTER 2

Maulana Azad's Strong Opposition to the Partition of India

Maulana Azad fought tooth and nail against partition of India along with his contemporary freedom fighters and stalwarts of the country's freedom struggle but succumbed to the political compulsion with a heavy heart. Following statements of Maulana clearly reflect his mindset.

Maulana Azad had said:

"I am a Muslim and profoundly conscious of the fact that I have inherited Islam's glorious tradition of the last fourteen hundred years. I am not prepared to loose even a small part of that legacy. The history and teachings of Islam, its arts and letters, its culture and civilisation are part of my wealth and it is my duty to cherish and guard them...But, with all these feelings, I have another equally deep realisation, born out of my life's experience which is strengthened and not hindered by the Islamic spirit. I am equally proud of the fact that I am an Indian, an essential part of the indivisible unity of the Indian nationhood, a vital factor in its total makeup, without which this noble edifice will remain incomplete."

"If the whole world is our country and is to be honoured, the dust of India has the first place...If all mankind are our brothers, then the Indians have the first place."

To Maulana India meant only undivided India and a unified nation, not a partitioned India and a divided nation.

The following extract from Maulana Azad's historic Presidential Address to the 53rd session of the Indian National Congress at Ramgarh, 1940 also speaks of his political acumen, strong opposition to the partition of India and firm belief that minorities shall get full protection in undivided India and that it was absurd for them to be apprehensive about their rights and interests in a democratic India. But his assurances, his eloquence as a great orator and strong advocacy for unified India happened to be a louse not to move on the ears of the emotional supporters of Jinnah's two-nation theory and his entire political exercise proved to be futile and his political discourse proved to be heedless for this class of people as they were quite apprehensive of their future in unified India probably on the premise that minority can never prevail against or surmount majority and they shall ever remain subdued.

"Friends,

In 1923 you elected me President of this National Assembly. For the second time, after seventeen years, you have once again conferred upon me the same honour. Seventeen years is not a long period in the history of national struggles. But now the pace of events and world change is so rapid that our old standards no longer apply. During these last seventeen years we have passed through many stages, one after another. We had a long journey before us, and it was inevitable that we should pass through several stages.

We rested at many a point no doubt, but never stopped. We surveyed and examined every prospect; but we were not ensnared by it, and passed on. We faced many ups and downs, but always our faces were turned towards the goal. The world may have doubted our intentions and determination, but we never had a moment's doubt. Our path was full of difficulties, and at every step we were faced with great obstacles. It may be that we did not proceed as rapidly as we desired, but we did not flinch from marching forward.

If we look back upon the period between 1923 and 1940, 1923 will appear to us a faded landmark in the distance. In 1923, we desired to reach our goal; but the goal was so distant then that even the milestones were hidden from our eyes. Raise your eyes today and look ahead. Not only do you see the milestones clearly, but the goal itself is not distant. But this is evident: that nearer we get to the goal, the more intense does our struggle become. Although the rapid march of events has taken us farther from our old landmark and brought us nearer our goal, yet it has created new troubles and difficulties for us. Today our caravan is passing a very critical stage. The essential difficulty of such a critical period lies in its conflicting possibilities. It is very probable that a correct step may bring us very near our goal; and on the other hand, a false step may land us in fresh troubles and difficulties.

Since war began, several members of the British Cabinet have tried to make the world believe that the old order of British imperialism has ended, and that today the British nation has no other aims except those of peace and justice. Which country could have more warmly acclaimed such a declaration than India? But the fact is that in spite of these declarations, British imperialism stands in the way of peace and justice today exactly as it did before the War. The Indian demand was the touchstone for all such claims. They were so tested, and found to be counterfeit and untrue.

The Minorities and the Political Future of India

For a hundred and fifty years British imperialism has pursued the policy of divide and rule, and by emphasising internal differences, sought to use various groups for the consolidation of its own power. That was the inevitable result of India's political subjection, and it is folly for us to complain and grow bitter. A foreign government can never encourage internal unity in the subject country, for disunity is the surest guarantee for the continuance of its own domination.

But when we were told, and the world was asked to believe, that British Imperialism had ended, and the long chapter of Indian History dominated by it had closed, was it unreasonable for us to expect that British statesmen would at last give up this evil inheritance and not exploit the communal situation for political ends? But the time for this is yet distant; we may not cling to such vain hopes. So the last five months with their succession of events have established. Imperialism, in spite of all assurances to the contrary, still flourishes; it has yet to be ended.

But whatever the roots of our problems might be, it is obvious that India, like other countries, has her internal problems. Of these, the communal problem is an important one. We do not and cannot expect the British Government to deny its existence. The communal problem is undoubtedly with us; and if we want to go ahead, we must need take it into account. Every step that we take by ignoring it will be a wrong step. The problem is there; to admit its existence, however, does not mean that it should be used as a weapon against India's national freedom. British Imperialism has always exploited it to this end. If Britain desires to end her imperialistic methods in India and close that dismal chapter of history, then the first signs of this change must naturally appear in her treatment of the communal problem.

The entire history of the Congress demonstrates that it has always acknowledged the existence of the problem…

It has always held to two basic principles in this connection, and every step was taken deliberately with these in view.

1. Whatever constitution is adopted for India, there must be the fullest guarantees in it for the rights and interests of minorities.
2. The minorities should judge for themselves what safeguards are necessary for the protection of their rights and interests. The majority should not decide this. Therefore, the decision in this respect must depend upon the consent of the minorities and not on a majority vote.

The question of the minorities is not a special Indian problem. It has existed in other parts of the world. I venture to address the world from this platform, and to enquire whether any more just and more equitable course of action can be adopted in this connection, than the one suggested above? If so, what is it? Is there anything lacking in this approach?

Dissensions were sown and encouraged amongst us, and yet we are taunted because of them. We are told to put an end to our communal conflicts, but opportunity to do so is denied to us. Such is the position deliberately created to thwart us; such are the chains that bind. But no difficulties or constraints can deter us from taking the right steps with courage and fortitude. Our path is full of obstacles, but we are determined to overcome them.

The Muslims of India and the Future of India

We have considered the problem of the minorities of India. But are the Muslims such a minority as to have the least doubt or fear about their future? A small minority may legitimately have fears and apprehensions, but can the Muslims allow themselves to be disturbed by them? I do not know how many of you are familiar with my writings, twenty-eight years ago, in the Al-Hilal. If there are any such here, I would request them to refresh their memories. Even then I gave expression to my conviction, and I repeat this today, that in the texture of Indian Politics, nothing is further removed from the truth than to say that Indian Muslims occupy the position of a political minority.

It is equally absurd for them to be apprehensive about their rights and interests in a democratic India. This fundamental mistake has opened the door to countless misunderstandings. False arguments were built up on wrong premises. This error, on the one hand, brought confusion into the minds of Musalmans about their own true position; and, on the other hand, it involved the world in misunderstandings, so that the picture of India could not be seen in the right perspective.

If time had permitted, I would have told you in detail how during the last sixty years, this artificial and untrue picture of India was made, and whose hands traced it. In effect, this was the result of the same policy of divide and rule which took particular shape in the minds of British Officialdom in India after the Congress launched the national movement. The object of this was to prepare the Musalmans for use against the new political awakening. In this plan, prominence was given to two points.

First, that India was inhabited by two different communities, the Hindus and the Musalmans, and for this reason no demand could be made in the name of a united nation. Second, that numerically the Musalmans were far less than the Hindus; and because of this, the necessary consequence of the establishment of democratic institutions in India would be to establish the rule of the Hindu majority and to jeopardize the existence of the Muslims. I shall not go into any greater detail now. Should you, however, wish to know the early history of this matter, I would refer you to the time of Lord Dufferin, a former Viceroy of India, and Sir Auckland Colvin, a former Lieutenant Governor of the N.W.P., now the United Provinces.

Thus, were sown the seeds of disunity by British Imperialism on Indian soil. The plant grew and was nurtured and spread its nettles; and even though fifty years have passed since then, the roots are still there.

Politically speaking, the word minority does not mean just a group that is so small in number and so lacking in other qualities that give strength, that it has no confidence in its own capacity to protect itself from the much larger group that surrounds it. It is not enough that the group should be relatively the smaller, but that it should be absolutely so small as to be incapable of protecting its interests. Thus, this is not merely a question of numbers; other factors count also. If a country has two major groups numbering a million and two millions respectively, it does not necessarily follow that because one is half the other, therefore it must call itself politically a minority and consider itself weak.

If this is the right test, let us apply it to the position of the Muslims in India. You will see at a glance a vast concourse, spreading out all over the country; they stand erect, and to imagine that they exist helplessly as a "minority" is to delude oneself.

The Muslims in India number between eighty and ninety millions. The same type of social or racial divisions which affect other communities do not divide them. The powerful bonds of Islamic brotherhood and equality have protected them to a large extent from the weakness that flows from social divisions. It is true that they number only one-fourth of the total population; but the question is not one of population ratio, but of the large numbers and the strength behind them. Can such a vast mass of humanity have any legitimate reason for apprehension that in a free and democratic India, it might be unable to protect its rights and interest?

These numbers are not confined to any particular area, but spread out unevenly over different parts of the country. In four provinces out of eleven in India there is a Muslim majority, the other religious groups being minorities. If British Baluchistan is added, there are five provinces with [a] Muslim majority. Even if we are compelled at present to consider this question on the basis of religious groupings, the position of the Muslims is not that of a minority only. If they are in a minority in seven provinces, they are in a majority in five. This being so, there is absolutely no reason why they should be oppressed by the feeling of being a minority.

Whatever may be the details of the future constitution of India, we know that it will be an all-India federation which is in the fullest sense democratic, and every unit of which will have autonomy in regard to internal affairs. The federal centre will be concerned only with all-India matters of common concern, such as foreign relations, defence, customs, etc. Under these circumstances, can anyone who has any conception of the actual working of a democratic constitution, allow himself to be led astray by this false issue of majority and minority?

I cannot believe for an instant that there can be any room whatever for these misgivings in the picture of India's future. These apprehensions are arising because, in the words of a British statesman regarding Ireland, we are yet standing on the banks of the river and, though wishing to swim, are unwilling to enter the water. There is only one remedy: we should take the plunge fearlessly. No sooner is this done then we shall realise that all our apprehensions were without foundation.

A Basic Question for Indian Musalmans

It is now nearly thirty years since I first attempted to examine this question as an Indian Musalman. The majority of the Muslims then were keeping completely apart from the political struggle, and they were influenced by the same mentality of aloofness and antagonism which prevailed amongst them previously in the year 1888. This depressing atmosphere did not prevent me from giving my anxious thought to this matter, and I reached quickly a final conclusion, which influenced my belief and action. I saw India, with all her many burdens, marching ahead to her future destiny. We were fellow-passengers in this boat and we could not ignore its swift passage through the waters; and so it became necessary for us to come to a clear and final decision about our plan of action. How were we to do so?

Not merely by skimming the surface of the problem, but by going down to its roots, and then to consider our position. I did so, and I realised that the solution of the whole problem depended on the answer to one question: Do we, Indian Musalmans, view the free India of the future with suspicion and distrust, or with courage and confidence? If we view it with fear and suspicion, then undoubtedly we have to follow a different path. No present declaration, no promise for the future, no constitutional safeguards, can be a remedy for our doubts and fears. We are then forced to tolerate the existence of a third power. This third power is already entrenched here and has no intention of withdrawing; and if we follow this path of fear, we must need look forward to its continuance.

But if we are convinced that for us fear and doubt have no place, and that we must view the future with courage and confidence in ourselves, then our course of action becomes absolutely clear. We find ourselves in a new world, which is free from the dark shadows of doubt, vacillation, inaction, and apathy, and where the light of faith and determination, action and enthusiasm, never fails. The confusions of the times, the ups and downs that come our way, the difficulties that beset our thorny path, cannot change the direction of our steps. It becomes our bounden duty then to march with assured steps to India's national goal.

I arrived at this definite conclusion without the least hesitation, and every fibre of my being revolted against the former alternative. I could not bear the thought of it. I could not conceive it possible for a Musalman to tolerate this, unless he has rooted out the spirit of Islam from every corner of his being.

I started the Al-Hilal in 1912, and put this conclusion of mine before the Muslims of India. I need not remind you that my cries were not without effect. The period from 1912 to 1918 marked a new phase in the political awakening of the Muslims. Towards the end of 1920, on my release after four years of internment, I found that the political ideology of the Musalmans had broken through its old mould and was taking another shape. Twenty years have gone by and much has happened since then. The tide of events has ever risen higher, and fresh waves of thought have enveloped us. But this fact still remains unchanged: that the general opinion amongst the Muslims is opposed to going back.

That is certain; they are not prepared to retrace their steps. But again, they are full of doubts about their future path. I am not going into the reasons for this; I shall only try to understand the effects. I would remind my co-religionists that today I stand exactly where I stood in 1912 when I addressed them on this issue. I have given thought to all those innumerable occurrences which have happened since then; my eyes have watched them, my mind has pondered over them.

These events did not merely pass me by; I was in the midst of them, a participant, and I examined every circumstances with care. I cannot be false to what I have myself seen and observed; I cannot quarrel with my own convictions; I cannot stifle the voice of my conscience. I repeat today what I have said throughout this entire period: that the ninety millions of Muslims of India have no other right course of action than the one to which I invited them in 1912.

Some of my co-religionists, who paid heed to my call in 1912, are in disagreement with me today. I do not wish to find fault with them, but I would make appeal to their sincerity and sense of responsibility. We are dealing with the destinies of peoples and nations. We cannot come to right conclusions if we are swept away by the passions of the moment. We must base our judgments on the solid realities of life. It is true that the sky is overcast today, and the outlook is dark. The Muslims have to come into the light of reality. Let them examine every aspect of the matter again today, and they will find no other course of action open to them.

The Musalmans and a 'United Nation'

I am a Musalman and am proud of that fact. Islam's splendid traditions of thirteen hundred years are my inheritance. I am unwilling to lose even the smallest part of this inheritance. The teaching and history of Islam, its arts and letters and civilisation, are my wealth and my fortune. It is my duty to protect them.

As a Musalman I have a special interest in Islamic religion and culture, and I cannot tolerate any interference with them. But in addition to these sentiments, I have others also which the realities and conditions of my life have forced upon me. The spirit of Islam does not come in the way of these sentiments; it guides and helps me forward.

I am proud of being an Indian. I am a part of the indivisible unity that is Indian nationality. I am indispensable to this noble edifice, and without me this splendid structure of India is incomplete. I am an essential element which has gone to build India. I can never surrender this claim.

It was India's historic destiny that many human races and cultures and religions should flow to her, finding a home in her hospitable soil, and that many a caravan should find rest here. Even before the dawn of history, these caravans trekked into India, and wave after wave of newcomers followed. This vast and fertile land gave welcome to all, and took them to her bosom.

One of the last of these caravans, following the footsteps of its predecessors, was that of the followers of Islam.

This came here and settled here for good.

This led to a meeting of the culture-currents of two different races. Like the Ganga and Jumuna, they flowed for a while through separate courses, but nature's immutable law them together and joined them in a sangam. This fusion was a notable event in history. Since then, destiny, in her own hidden way, began to fashion a new India in place of the old. We brought our treasures with us, and India too was full of the riches of her own precious heritage. We gave our wealth to her, and she unlocked the doors of her own treasures to us. We gave her what she needed most, the most precious of gifts from Islam's treasury, the message of democracy and human equality.

Full eleven centuries have passed by since then. Islam has now as great a claim on the soil of India as Hinduism. If Hinduism has been the religion of the people here for several thousands of years, Islam also has been their religion for a thousand years. Just as a Hindu can say with pride that he is an Indian and follows Hinduism, so also we can say with equal pride that we are Indians and follow Islam. I shall enlarge this orbit still further. The Indian Christian is equally entitled to say with pride that he is an Indian and is following a religion of India, namely Christianity.

Eleven hundred years of common history have enriched India with our common achievement. Our languages, our poetry, our literature, our culture, our art, our dress, our manners and customs, the innumerable happenings of our daily life, everything bears the stamp of our joint endeavour. There is indeed no aspect of our life which has escaped this stamp. Our languages were different, but we grew to use a common language; our manners and customs were dissimilar, but they acted and reacted on each other, and thus produced a new synthesis. Our old dress may be seen only in ancient pictures of bygone days; no one wears it today.

This joint wealth is the heritage of our common nationality, and we do not want to leave it and go back to the times when this joint life had not begun. If there are any Hindus amongst us who desire to bring back the Hindu life of a thousand years ago and more, they dream, and such dreams are vain fantasies. So also if there are any Muslims who wish to revive their past civilisation and culture, which they brought a thousand years ago from this thousand years of our joint life has moulded us into a common nationality. This cannot be done artificially. Nature does her fashioning through her hidden processes in the course of centuries. The cast has now been moulded and destiny has set her seal upon it. Whether we like it or not, we have now become an Indian nation, united and indivisible. No fantasy or artificial scheming to separate and divide can break this unity. We must accept the logic of fact and history, and engage ourselves in the fashioning of our future destiny————."

Can there be any other authentic proof of his firm opposition to the partition of India than this objective statement of this great patriot and nationalist made before a very responsible audience? Can there be two opinions about it? Certainly not. This speech is the most reliable documentary proof of his being one of the strongest champions of an undivided India and a unified nation. He reconciled to the partition only under political compulsion and that, too, as the saddest person on the Indian soil. His aversions in his book '*India Wins Freedom*' Maulana also bear testimony to it. Maulana Azad had great regard for Nehru but he did not hesitate to criticise some of his actions. He was not happy with his press conference of 10th July 1946, which led to demise of May 16 Plan and carved the way for the Partition. He always appreciated his sincerity, political acumen and uprightness but the said conference was a sad and painful event for him.

In the latter part of the book released 30 years in 1988 Maulana once again retreated that "as a Muslim, I for one am not prepared for a moment to give up my right to treat the whole of India as my domain and share in the shaping of its political and economic life. To me it seems a sure sign of cowardice to give up what is my patrimony and content myself with a mere fragment of it."

CHAPTER 3

Views of Eminent National and International Figures about Maulana Azad

Maulana Azad's views about partition and views of persons of different shades have been contentious in both India and Pakistan. Many Pakistanis considered his ideas of secularism and nationalism to be against Islam but the bearded Maulanas with caps on their heads belonging to the then Deoband School of Thought supported him wholeheartedly and without any reservations, went to jail and suffered punishment during British rule. Likewise, some critics are of the view that he should have put in more efforts to stall the process of partition. Such an approach is not worth considering or appreciating as he had put in best efforts to stall it. Those who know Maulana or have read about him fully know that whatever he said or wrote he meant that. He was a stranger to hypocrisy though he was fully aware of the strange ways of hypocrites and could easily distinguish between serious and non-serious persons and could separate chaff from the grain. He had seen so many so called political chameleons changing their colours in pre-independence and post-independence India. Had he been on the other side, India's map could be or would have been different today but his steps never tottered and he remained firm throughout even in adverse and compelling situations though some of his contemporaries staggered and faltered on some occasions, may be under political compulsions or because of error in judgment. It would be a great folly to question the credentials of these great men-be Gandhi, Nehru, Patel or many other political celebrities and unsung heroes. However, we, the people of India, are at liberty to express our views freely under the Indian Constitution but this liberty is not unfettered as it is subject to imposition of reasonable restrictions for the sake of maintaining public order, decency or morality and above all integrity of the country and friendly relations with foreign countries.

Maulana Azad, who died on February 22, 1958 ranks among the top builders of modern India and among the top freedom fighters. He dedicated his entire life to liberate India from British colonial rule, and to promote unity among the Hindus and Muslims and for these reasons received high praise from Mahatma Gandhi and Jawaharlal Nehru. Maulana Azad was proud to be a Muslim and an Indian. He was not only enlightened, erudite, wise and humble, he was also a man who often led from the front and set personal examples for others. Much has been written about Azad in the last six decades. Today as we pay tribute to this great Indian patriot, he continues to live in the minds and hearts of his countrymen. Let us reflect on how some top Indian leaders viewed him, and what were his own views about India and the role of Muslims as an integral part of the Indian nation.

Mahatma Gandhi:

"Maulana Azad is the most forceful, truthful, and fearless *satyagrahi* (a participant in Gandhian way of non-violent action popularly known as non-violence or a way of life based on love and compassion) and fighter against oppression and injustice that I have come across. "Though I am grateful to all my companions, I would like to mention especially Maulana Abul Kalam Azad, whose erudition has delighted me incredibly, and has sometimes overwhelmed me. In Azad along with the good qualities of the past, the graciousness, the deep learning and tolerance, there is a strange and unique mixture of the urges of today and the modern outlook." "Maulana Azad was a very special representative in a high degree, of the great composite culture which has gradually grown in India. He represented the synthesis of various cultures which had flown in and lost themselves in the ocean of Indian life and humanity, affecting and changing them and being changed themselves by them. In that sense, I can hardly conceive of any other person who can replace him, because the age which produced him is past."

Maulana Azad's Own Views: "I am a Muslim and profoundly conscious of the fact that I have inherited Islam's glorious tradition of the last fourteen hundred years. I am not prepared to loose even a small part of that legacy. The history and teachings of Islam, its arts and letters, its culture and civilisation are part of my wealth and it is my duty to cherish and guard them......But, with all these feelings, I have another equally deep realisation, born out of my life's experience which is strengthened and not hindered by the Islamic spirit. I am equally proud of the fact that I am an Indian, an essential part of the indivisible unity of the Indian nationhood, a vital factor in its total makeup, without which this noble edifice will remain incomplete."

"If the whole world is our country and is to be honoured, the dust of India has the first place..........If all mankind are our brothers, then the Indians have the first place." "Not only is our national freedom impossible without Hindu-Muslim unity, we also can not create without it, the primary principles of humanity. If an angel were to tell me: "Discard Hindu-Muslim unity and within 24 hours I will give freedom to India"; I would prefer Hindu-Muslim unity. For the delay in the attainment of freedom will be a loss to India alone, but if the Hindu-Muslim unity disappears, that will be a loss to the whole humanity." "It was India's historic destiny that many human races, cultures, and religions should flow to her, and that many a caravan should find rest here........One of the last of these caravans was that of the followers of Islam. This came here and settled for good. In India everything bears the stamp of the joint endeavours of the Hindus and Muslims. Our languages were different, but we grew to use a common language. Our manners and customs were dissimilar, but they produced a new synthesis. No fantasy or artificial scheming to separate and divide us can break this unity."

Maulana Azad's views about his own attributes corroborate the views of Gandhi as quoted above.

The following extract from Nehru's Speech in Lok Sabha on the death of Maulana Abul Kalam Azad, February 24, 1958 is an absolutely objective assessment of this great son of India:

"MR. SPEAKER, SIR: It has fallen to my lot often to refer in this House to the death of a colleague or a great man. I have to perform that sad duty again today in regard to one who was with us a few days ago and who passed away rather suddenly, producing a sense of deep sorrow and grief not only to his colleagues in Parliament but to innumerable people all over the country.

It has become almost a commonplace, when a prominent person passes away, to say that he is irreplaceable. That is often true; yet I believe that it is literally and absolutely true in regard to the passing away of Maulana Azad. We have had great men and we will have great men, but I do submit that the peculiar and special type of greatness which Maulana Azad represented is not likely to be reproduced in India or anywhere else.

I need not refer to his many qualities, his deep learning, his scholarship and his great oratory. He was a great writer. He was great in many ways. He combined in himself the greatness of the past with the greatness of the present. He always reminded me of the great men of several hundred years ago about whom I have; read in history, the great men of the Renaissance, or in a later period, the encyclopaedists who preceded the French Revolution, men of intellect and men of action. He reminded also of what might be called the great quality of olden days—the graciousness, a certain courtesy or tolerance or patience which we sadly seek in the world today.

Even though we may seek to reach the moon, we do it with a lack of graciousness or of tolerance or of some things which have made life worth-while since life began. It was the strange and unique mixture of the good qualities of the past, the graciousness, the deep learning and toleration, and the urges of today which made Maulana Azad what he was.

Everyone knows that even in his early teens he was filled with the passion for freeing India and he turned towards ways even of violent revolution. Soon after he realised that violence was not the way which would gain results.

Maulana Azad was a very special representative in a high degree of the great composite culture which had gradually grown in India. He, in his own venue, in Delhi or in Bengal where he spent the greater part of his life, represented this synthesis of various cultures which had flowed in and lost themselves in the ocean of Indian life and humanity, affecting and changing them and being changed themselves by them. He came to represent more specially the culture of India as influenced by the cultures of the nations of Western Asia, namely, the Persian culture and the Arabic culture which have affected India for thousands of years. In that sense, I can hardly conceive of any other person who can replace him, because the age which produced him is past. A few of us have some faint idea of that age which is past.

Change is essential lest we should become rooted to some past habit. But I cannot help expressing a certain feeling of regret that with the bad, the good of the past days is also swept away and that good was eminently represented by Maulana Azad.

We mourn today the passing of a great man, a man of luminous intelligence and mighty intellect with an amazing capacity to pierce through a problem to its core. The word "luminous" is perhaps the best word I can use about his mind. When we miss and when we part with such a companion, friend, colleague, comrade, leader and teacher, there is inevitably a tremendous void created in our life and activities."

Nehru had also said:

"We have had great men and we will have great men, but I do submit that the peculiar and special type of greatness which Maulana Azad represented is not likely to be reproduced in India or anywhere else."

Narendra Modi

Chief Minister Narendra Modi and the Bharatiya Janata Party's prime ministerial candidate for the 2014 general elections, presently the Prime Minister of India, had expressed the following views about Maulana Azad and others but we are quoting here his views exclusively about Maulana Azad:

"He expressed his deep anguish over certain sections of society reducing stalwarts of the country's freedom struggle to mere partisan political leaders."

Writing in his blog on the occasion of the 125th birth anniversaries of Maulana Abul Kalam Azad and Acharya J B Kripalani, Modi said: "It is with deep anguish that I see how some of our friends have reduced stalwarts of the freedom struggle to mere partisan political leaders. There can be no greater disservice to our history than viewing these stalwarts through the narrow prism of political partisanship."

Stating that it is high time to realise that these leaders transcended barriers of caste, community, creed or party lines, Modi said: "Their ideals and legacy are not for any party, but for the entire nation to get inspired."

"What is equally worrying is the tendency of "speculative history" where some celebrity historians have appropriated to themselves the authority to speculate what some historical figure would have said or done," he added.

Referring specifically to the relations between Azad and Sardar Vallabhbhai Patel, the Gujarat Chief Minister said: "Yes, it is a fact that both Maulana Azad and Sardar Patel differed on many issues. But, it is equally a fact that both were guided by their absolute love and devotion for India, and both of them worked together on several occasions under the guidance of Mahatma Gandhi."

Of Maulana Abul Kalam Azad, he said he was blessed with a revolutionary streak from a young age, and did not hesitate to attack and criticise India's colonial rulers.

"He occupied an important place in the Congress party. He served as India's first Education Minister. Maulana Azad will also be remembered for his steadfast opposition to partition of India," said Modi. (Gandhinagar (Gujarat), Nov.11 (ANI) Gujarat)

Sarojini Naidu

"Do not talk of Maulana's age. He was 50 when he was born."

U. N. Dhebar

"Maulana Azad was an open book for anybody to read.......His eyes, the characteristic waving of hands, in fact his whole being spoke simultaneously. You could see behind every word that he uttered the faith and conviction of the great responsibility."

J. B. Kripalani

"Though he guided the crowd, he was shy of it; he was not of it. Gandhji influenced many aristocrats by birth or position to rub shoulders with the crowd in those days. But the Maulana remained his own self, an aristocratic individual who viewed the crowd with indulgence from his great eminence."

Raj Gopal Gandhi

"Azad the orator could move an audience almost as effectively as Azad the writer. All over India people heard him, and one of his many speeches recruited for the national cause was a young man in Bihar called Jayaprakash Narayan."

Rasheed Ahmed Siddiqui

"Abul Kalam Azad was an era in his own self and as such he remained controversial for the unchanging ones who preferred to walk in the beaten path."

Syed Suleiman Nadvi

"Maulana Abul Kalam has refreshed our memory and reminded us of *jihad* which we had completely forgotten."

Press releases on Maulana Azad's death

"——It was by remarkable irony of fate that the learned Islamic divine with a scholarly commentary on Koran and many theological works to his credit should be in the forefront of Congress repudiation of 'two-nation theory' and the demand for

Pakistan, while the leader of the Muslim League should be highly westernised and unorthodox Jinnah——-" London Times.

"To him communal politics was anathema, and he never wavered in his conviction that people of all faiths in India-Hindus and Muslims, Sikhs and Christians-had to live as one community." The Ceylon Daily News.

When he was asked why he, a Mohammedan, should stand politically for that 'Hindu raj' which so many Muslims feared, instead of upholding the Islamic conception of Pakistan, he said that he could see no danger.

"Islam", he said, "has a strength far greater than that of any political arrangement and considerations of geographical boundaries would be utterly foreign to the doctrine of Mohammed."

"The true Muslim", he went on, "will by his deeds, his kindness and consideration, attract others to gather under his standard of truth."—The New York Times.

"——He was a great scholar and a champion of Islam who had devoted all his life to the freedom of his country. His memory was a rich treasure-house of all the best poetry of the East....... One felt in his company as if he was with one of Akbar's *nauratan*[1]......He belonged to the front line of those Muslim scholars who combined love for Islam with nationalism and achieve his aim be worked with the great leader of India. Gandhi——-" The Milliyet, Istanbul.

"The Maulana was valuable and precious not only for India but the Muslim world. In him the Turkish nation has lost a real." Dunya Istanbul.

"We shall always remember him as one of the greatest intellectuals of the Islamic world and a friend of Turkey,"— Celal Yardimici, Minister of Education, Turkey.

"His death is no doubt a great loss not only to India, but also to the Arab and Islamic world." Mustafa Sibal, Damascus.

"His death is a great loss to the world of literature, to the Islamic world, and to all thinkers in general. History would remember his great services to the ideological and scientific fields." Munir al-Qadhi, President Iraqi Academy.

"......Though a great leader of the freedom movement in India, (he) was one who belonged to the whole world. He was a great promoter of Indo-Iranian culture." The Pars-Iran.

"In him the Indian government and people of India have lost a great patriot and one of the ablest sons of India who devoted his whole life in the struggle for independence and to the building up of India as a strong national ally." Ho Chi Minh, President Republic of Vietnam.

"A renowned personality not only of India but of the whole of Asia"...Nepal Times.

"He did not need to cultivate convictions: he breathed them." The National Herald, Lucknow.

"His ardent patriotism, his deep scholarship and his robust thinking have been distinct assets in the political revolution of our times and his death has come as a national tragedy." The Hindustan Times.

"When the two nation theory became prominent, in Maulana Azad was symbolised the struggle to maintain the country intact," The Stateman.

"In the passing away of Maulana Azad the nation has lost a great statesman, a great scholar and a great patriot." The Times of India.

"Belonging to the aristocracy of intellect, he easily identified himself with people's movements." The National Herald, Lucknow.

Notes

1. Following nine persons were the *Nauratans* in Akbar's court:

   Abul Fazal

   Abul Fazal was the chronicler of Akbarnama, being in three volumes prepared in over seven years. Its third volume is titled as 'Ain-i-Akbari.'

   Faizi

   Faizi, a scholar in the philosophy and literature of Greece as well as Muslim theology. He was the poet laureate of Akbar.

   Miyan Tansen

   He was a court musician of Akbar.

   Raja Birbal

   He was the court jester. He was known for his intelligence and administrative and strategic acumen. He was also a poet.

   Raja Todar Mal

   Raja Todar Mal was Akbar's finance minister.

   Raja Man Singh

   Raja Man Singh was a trusted general in Akbar's army.

   Abul Rahim Khan-I-Khana

   He was known for his Hindi poetry.

   Fakir Aziao-Din

   He was a sufi mystic, and an advisor to the king.

   Mirza Aziz Koka

   He was one of the leading nobles and also foster brother of Akbar. He served as Subedar of Gujarat.

Chapter 4

Maulana's Major Works and Quotable Quotes

Major works, writings and speeches of Maulana Azad and quotations reflecting his intellectual acumen

Major works

- Tazkirah, Calcutta 1919.
- Azad ki Kahani Khud Azad ki Zabani, dictated to Malihabadi, Calcutta 1959.
- Ghubar-e-Khatir, Delhi, Hali Publishing House.
- India Wins Freedom, Orient Longman, 1959.
- Karavan-e-Khayal, Bijnor, 1946.

The following quotations from the writings and speeches of Maulana Azad reflecting his intellectual acumen, acuteness of mind, broadmindedness, objective approach and dynamism have not lost their relevance with the passage of time and many predictions made impliedly or explicitly in these quotations have withstood the test of time.

Ghubar-e-Khatir

'Ghubar-e-Khatir' is one of the most important works of Maulana Abul Azad, written primarily during 1942 to1946 when he was imprisoned in Ahmednagar Fort in Maharashtra during British Rule, being in the form of collection of 24 letters, addressed to his friend Maulana Habibur Rahman Khan Sherwani. Ghubar-e-Khatir perhaps means in English "Salliies of Mind" "Dust of a Pensive Heart" or "Mist of the Pensive Heart." It is the blending of Urdu prose and Persian verse.The collection of letters was named Ghubar-e-Khatir by Azad, the title of which he borrowed from the work of an eighteenth century Indo-Persian poet, Mir Azmatullah Bekhabar Bilgerami. Azad has used quite a number of Persian verses in his letters. The Persian verses in the letters of Ghubar-e-Khatir contained verses of eminent Persian poets and Indo-Persian literature. He had quoted Hafiz, Khosro, Faizi and a host of others. Maulana Azad did not adopt stereotype approach in using, applying and interpreting these verses. He adopted pragmatic approach keeping in view the context which at times differed from their literal interpretation.

"My life is an open book.........I am selfless, a person *sans* any selfish motive. A selfless person is boundless. Do you know who is boundless? I know your answer will be 'No'. I will let you know. A boundless person is one against whom even a sword becomes inefficacious, that is, he cannot be handled violently."

"I feel that my nature, habits, manners, behaviour, disposition, taste, asthetic sense etc. do reflect my family background. I owe it all to my paternal and maternal parents. Both of them have been the stereotyped victims of centuries old orthodoxy."

"——Having reached a particular stage, I got rid of my legacy (orthodoxy all around) and demolished the old structure to raise the new one."

"Sometimes, like unseasonal flowers, untimely change also occurs in one's temperament. It may be attributed to nature or anachronism (error in regard to time) but it does happen."

"........To be happy is not merely a physical requirement; it is our moral responsibility. Live and let live happily. Do not feel depressed otherwise others will follow suit."

"I never allow my heart to sink; I remain firm even in compelling situation(s). It is the key to my success in every walk of life."

"Change in life, be it positive or otherwise, has its own significance."

"If you take up some work, keep going till it is finished."

Tazkirah

Tazkirah is another book of Maulana Azad wherein he speaks of his life, outlook, thinking and philosophy speaking in Urdu and relates it to beautiful Persian poetry.

Karavan-e-khayal

The work is the treasure of his views about this world, the life in it and the values he cherished as also his objective approach and dynamism.

"Generally people attain the age of discretion and become mature after completing 21/22 years of their life but by grace of God I reached this stage when I was just 13/14 year old."

"...A purposeless life is no life. One must have some mission in life."

The following quotation from his speech (also containing author's comments) delivered at the All India Educational Conference held in January,1948 further reveal as to how foresighted he was and how pragmatic his approach was.

While addressing the All India Educational Conference, New Delhi, January 1948, Maulana had dealt with the following subjects, issues and problems and expressed his views:

1. **Basic Education—a birth right**

   "It is the birth right of every individual to receive at least the basic education without which he cannot fully discharge his duties as a citizen. (Speeches)

   A twelve point programme of social education—particularly in villages—was announced by the Maulana on May 31, 1948.

2. **New Techniques of Mass Education**

   "......modern science has placed in our hands effective instruments in the form of broadcasting and the film. I am considering schemes by which they may be utilised to the fullest extent for broadening the mind of the masses and opening up a new world of knowledge to them." (Speeches)

3. **Aim of Education—Development of International Outlook**

   "Do not forget that you can seal all your worldly possessions within national and geographical limits but no seal can be put on learning and civilisation......In the advancement of nations there is no greater hindrance than narrow mindedness. In the domain of religion it appears in the form of blind faith and wants to deceive us in the name of orthodoxy. In politics it wants to over power us in the gules of nationalism. In learning and culture it makes an appeal to us in the name of our nation and country...the nationalism propagated in the nineteenth century Europe is all shattered and the world is sick of the bounds of narrow nationalism...Instead of a small cooped up nationalities the world wants to build super nationalism. We shall find a secure place in the comity of nations only if we are international minded and tolerant. (Speeches)

4. Necessary of Fundamental Research

"…..there can be no advance in other industry or technology without fundamental research work. The scope of such research should however, be extended and cover not only the scientific subjects but also the humanities, including philosophy, the social sciences, anthropology etc." (Speeches)

5. Role of the English Language

"The greatest advantage that we gained from the adoption of English… it has led to the unification of the whole country. It is the connecting link between all the Provincial Governments, universities, Legislative assemblies, public platforms and national organisations…India's position and recognition in the international world are greatly due to our having recourse to the English language both written and spoken." (Speeches)

6. Scientific Terminology

"……The Central Advisor Board has (declared) that scientific terms are international, and it would be a serious mistake to try to translate them. I agree with the view of the Board and believe that this is the only rational solution of the difficulty." (Speeches)

Note: This difficulty has since been removed and Commission for scientific and technical terminology is doing a good job. It has prepared many a glossary of scientific and technical terms.

7. Indian Philosophy

"I think that with the exception of two specific branches of learning (Aristotle's Logic and Ptolemy's Majestic) the Indian mind has shown itself superior in every respect to the achievements of the Greeks. We therefore need a new history of Philosophy in which Philosophy may find its rightful place." (Speeches)

8. Reorientation of Historical Approach

"All histories used in our Universities today...... suffer both from lacunae and distortions. Nothing is more important today than the reorientation of historical studies." (Speeches)

9. Study of Oriental and Asiatic Languages

"We must not forget that in the past. India was a centre where the currents of Asiatic thought met and from which flowed out streams which spread to the farthest corner of the Asiatic continent. To appreciate Ancient India truly it is therefore essential to have a knowledge and understanding of other Asiatic languages and cultures as well." (Speeches)

10. Religious Education

"At first it was considered that religions would stand in the way of the free intellectual development of a child but now it has been admitted that religions cannot altogether be dispensed with...in India we cannot have an intellectual mould without religion." (Speeches)

11. Social Education

"...Preparation of plans for imparting social education to the Indian people...Social education may therefore be defined as a course of study towards the production of a consciousness of citizenship among the people and the promotion of social solidarity among them." (Speeches)

12. Education of Women

"I need hardly say that all our educational programme will ultimately depend upon the proper education of women. If women take to education, more than half of our problems will be solved." (Speeches)

13. Agriculture and Education

"A hard fact which we must face is that the economic life of India is not properly balanced between agriculture and industry...Our present agricultural education is defective because it lacks adequate practical basis...Our general education especially in the earlier stages, must therefore give a greater importance to the theory and practice of agriculture." (Speeches)

14. Employment and Education

"It appears to me that increasing emphasis will be placed on providing higher education in the field of agriculture, medicine, engineering, technology and science." (Speeches)

"A good school is a national asset of the highest value at any place or at any time. Schools are the laboratories which produce the future citizens of a state. The quality of the state, therefore, depends upon the quality of such laboratories." (Speech at Scindia School, Gwalior)

"Urdu is the product of this country. Why have we become so narrow minded? This narrow mindedness may prove fatal for such persons. Urdu is not the language of the followers of any particular religion. Even if it is admitted that it is the language of the Muslims, will it be something objectionable to provide assistance (financial) to an Urdu institution." (an extract from his speech made in the Parliament)

"Hindi has got its rightful place. We should admit it but Urdu must also get its due." (an extract from his last speech made on February 15, 1998)

CHAPTER 5

Maulana's Views on Partition (in the form of a monologue, that is, a presumptive soliloquy)

Monologue

(Speaker being Maulana Azad and audience being pre-partition Muslims of India)

Can a person with his western lifestyle, with no knowledge of Islamic tenets and practices (otherwise a very learned man) having received education in England, acclimatized with English traditions and culture, not knowing Urdu, a language which supporters of Pakistan are promising to declare official language of that country, a man asking his personal assistant what is *fateha* (the opening chapter, or exordium of Quran recited generally as a prayer for the departed souls.) can be your leader? You are listening his speeches without understanding as to what he is saying. Is it not blind following? Just think about the life of escapism you are opting for, in the sacred name of *Hijrat* (migration). Get into the habit of exercising your own brains, and strengthening your own hearts. If you do so, only then will you realise how immature your decisions are. You will become *mahajir* (one who quits his/her country, especially on public calamity or persecution) in your own country and Punjabis and Sindhis will never accept you as sons of the soil. Is there any situation like public calamity or persecution here in India? If India is divided into two states there would remain three and half crores of Muslims scattered in small minorities all over India, 17 per cent in UP, 12 per cent in Bihar and 9 per cent in Madras. Thus, you will become weaker in the Hindu majority provinces. Constitutionally you may be at par in the proposed state, but practically you will be treated as a separate group or species different from others. These two countries will continue to fight with each other at the cost of their development. Eastern part of proposed Pakistan can never remain integrated with Pakistan for geographical, cultural and linguistic reasons. Punjabi lobby will dominate Bengalis and they will feel subdued. The result would be uprising and reprisal from the other side and Pakistan will disintegrate.

Do you know that Jinnah is using religion for political ends as he is neither a devoted Muslim nor a true follower of Islam. He does not know as to how *namaz* (prayers) is offered. He is left with no other choice but to do so as he cannot accept his No. 2 or even lower position in Congress. At one stage, he was the champion of Hindu-Muslim unity, but now his advocacy for partition/ Pakistan is the only alternative for his political survival as he can never attain the high status of Quaid-e-Azam in India in the presence of Gandhi, Nehru, Patel or anyone else. I cannot reconcile to the idea of partition at any cost. For you, it is also *serate mustaqeem* (the right path). You must know that partition would be a major loss and disaster to Muslims on both sides. As regards India, Muslims will become absolute minority and as regards Pakistan, Muslim population of Pakistan shall never be able to face a giant like India in all sectors and areas at all international fora. Will it be a healthy situation for you or a solution of your problems? You might be thinking that in case of unified India Hindu majority will harass you and interfere in

Muslim majority provinces. Don't be afraid of it. (He, probably keeping into his mind the provisions of the Cabinet Mission Plan opined that "the Congress meets this fear by granting full autonomy to the provinces. It has also provided for two lists of central subjects, one compulsory and the other optional so that if any provincial unit so wants, it can administer all subjects itself except a minimum delegated to the Centre. The Congress scheme, therefore, ensures that Muslim majority provinces are internally free to develop as they will, but can at the same time influence the Centre on all issues which affect India as a whole, as so quoted by Asghar Ali Engineer in his article published on August 15, 2010). I assure you that the centre will not override the powers of Muslim majority provinces. Ponder over it.

Chapter 6

Maulana's Views on Hindu Muslim Unity

In a speech at a special session of the Indian National Congress in 1923, Maulana had said:

"If an angel were to descend from the clouds today and settle on Delhi's Qutab Minar and proclaim that India can win Swaraj (self-rule) within two hours provided that India renounces Hindu-Muslim unity, then I would renounce Swaraj and not unity. Because if Swaraj is delayed that is a loss to India, but if unity is lost that is a loss to humanity."

Azad, being a firm believer in Indian nationalism and Hindu-Muslim unity, had vehemently opposed the idea of the partition till the last moment. He used to tell those championing the cause of Pakistan that "If you go to Pakistan, you might find your co-religionists, but never your countrymen."

Mahatma Gandhi wrote, "Maulana Abul Kalam Azad has very considerately sent me a copy of his Press message on the Hindu-Muslim question. He is one of the very few men who may be claimed to be sincerely desirous to attain unity. He has asked me to call a meeting of the Working Committee in order to consider the question. I am not doing so before the Congress week at Cawnpore because the annual function is too near to warrant an earlier meeting of the Working Committee. I wish the Committee could discover a solution of the problem. But I must frankly confess that I despair. That is not to say that I despair of a solution altogether. I despair of the Congress discovering and enforcing a solution. Let us not conceal from ourselves the truth that the Congress does not represent the fighters in either camp. Not till those unseen ones who are behind the fighters are under the Congress influence and the newspaper editors who are fomenting dissensions are either converted to the unity doctrine or cease to have any influence, can the Congress do any useful work in the direction of unity. My bitter experience has taught me that they who take the name of unity mean disunion. The atmosphere around us is as false as was the atmosphere in Europe at the time of the last War. The newspapers never told the truth. The representatives of their respective nations had made of laying a fine art. All was fair in War. The old formula of Jehovah thirsting for the blood even of children was revived in all its nakedness. And so it is today in what may be called a miniature war between Hindus and Muslims. We may lie and cheat for saving our faiths. This has been said to me not by one mouth but many. This, however, is no cause for the slightest despair. I know that the demon of disunion is at his last gasp. A lie has no bottom. Disunion is a lie. Even if it is sheer self-interest, it will bring about unity. I had hoped for disinterested unity. But I will welcome a unity based even on mutual interest. Only it will not come in the way suggested by the Maulana Saheb. It will come, when it does come, in a way perhaps least expected by us. God is the Master Trickster. He knows how to confound us, frustrate our 'knavish tricks'. He sends death when one least expects it. He sends life when we see no sign of it. Let us admit our abject helplessness, let us own that we are utterly defeated. Out of the dust of our humility will, I feel sure, be built up an impregnable citadel of unity. I am sorry I am unable to return a more encouraging answer to the Maulana's appeal. Let him take comfort from the fact that I share his desire for union with the same intensity that he will credit himself with. What does it matter if I feel unable to share his faith in his plan of achieving unity? I shall do nothing to hinder it. I shall pray for the success of every sincere effort in that direction. My ceasing to fret does not mean the unity is no longer an article of my creed. Let me re-declare my undying faith in it. For the sake of it I must renounce the privilege of being a maker of the unity that is coming. I have the wisdom to stand aside and wait when my interference can only disturb the wound without healing."

Young India, 26-11-1925

'Maulana Azad's call of Hindu Muslim unity was not merely a political metaphor'-Professor M. Saud Alam Qasmi'

Delivering Maulana Abul Kalam Azad Memorial Lecture at Department of Education, Aligarh Muslim University (AMU) organised to mark Maulana Abul Kalam Azad's 125th birth anniversary, Professor M. Saud Alam Qasmi paid rich tribute to him especially for his call for the Hindu Muslim unity and his views on national integration.

"The call of Hindu Muslim unity was not a political metaphor of Maulana Azad. It was his sincere view based on religious teachings and demands of humanity", Professor M. Saud Alam Qasmi said on the occasion which is celebrated as National Education Day.

"The British Government adopted the policy of divide and rule, and Maulana Azad perceived it as a factor that divided humanity. Maulana Azad opposed all forces that divided humanity on the basis of religion, caste, creed, politics and geography", he said.

He said that Maulana Azad was an erudite and multifaceted personality who left his impression in the history of India.

"Religion, literature and politics were main factors in the Development of Maulana Azad's personality and he used these principles for the uplift of society, freedom of the country and unity of mankind", he said.

Stating that divisive forces are still active in the country and creating hatred amongst various sections on the basis of region and religion, Professor Qasmi said, "People should not allow them to destroy the social and secular fabric of the country."

He pointed out that the destiny of the country is shaped in classrooms and it is the duty of the educational institutions to teach and train young minds in a way that they become true messengers of peace and tolerance. "This would be the real tribute to Maulana Azad", he said.

Tuesday November 12, 2013 6:58 PM, ummid.com News Network

All the quotations and relevant facts mentioned above clearly reveal that Maulana was not only a great champion of unified India but it was his life line. He had unshakeable conviction that the then leadership shall never reconcile to the idea of partition. However, his dream of incorporating provisions in the Constitution of India for providing protective cover to the minorities proved to be true at least to the extent of a constitutional safeguard to this vulnerable section of society. Part III of the Constitution bears testimony to it and is its documentary proof.

Chapter 7

Constitutional Mandate for Religious Harmony and National Integration

Minorities exist wherever there is a majority. Protection of minorities means protection of human rights. The degree of a nation being civilised is measured by its treatment of the minorities and other weaker sections of the society.

The Indian Constitution provides full protection to the religious and linguistic minorities without specifying the minorities. Prior to the analysis of these provisions it would be pertinent to go through conceptual history of the term 'minority. After partition of India on religious grounds, a new State (Pakistan) was carved out. During pre-partition days, Maulana Abul Kalam Azad, the father figure of the Indian National Movement, whose secular credentials do not require any proof or testimony, firmly believed in one nation and one community, that is, the Indian Nation and the Indian Community. According to him, there was nothing like a minority in the Indian Polity. Maulana Azad, while addressing Congress Session at Ramgarh in 1940, had made it clear in unequivocal terms that nothing was more misunderstood than the Muslims were being called a minority community in India. He advised them not to have any doubts or suspicion regarding their rights in undivided India. To Maulana, India meant only unpartitioned India. The Maulana had expressed these views at a time when Constituent Assembly of which he was a member, was discussing incorporation of provisions for affording protection to the minorities. The original proposal of the Advisory Committee in the Constituent Assembly had recommended that the minorities in every unit shall be protected in respect of their language, script and culture and no laws or regulations may be enacted that may operate oppressively or prejudicially in this respect. It is another thing that the word 'minority' was substituted by the words 'section of citizens'. Motilal Nehru Report of the year 1928 had expressed the view that protection should be afforded to the minorities but this Report, too, did not define the term 'minority'. Likewise, the Sapru Report of the year 1945 had used the words 'Minority Commission' but did not define the term. The U.N. Sub Commission on Prevention of Discrimination and Protection of Minorities has defined 'minority' as one including only those non-dominant groups in a population which possess and wish to preserve stable, ethnic, religious or linguistic traditions or characteristics markedly different from those of the population. It also mentions that such minorities should properly include a number of persons sufficient by themselves to preserve such traditions or characteristics, and that such minorities must be loyal and faithful to the State of which they are national. Article 27 of the International Covenant on Civil and Political Rights provides that in those States in which ethnic, religious or linguistic minorities exist, persons belonging to such minorities shall not be denied the right, in community with the other members of their group, to enjoy their own culture, to profess and practice their own religion, or to use their own language but the term 'minority' has not been defined in this Convention too.

It was after 43 years of the enforcement of the Constitution that by a Notification issued in 1993 under the National Commission for Minorities Act, 1992 the Muslims, Christians, Sikhs, Buddhists and Parsi Zoroastrians were notified as the 'minorities' at the national level for the purposes of the Act. In TMA Pai's case (2002), the Supreme Court has held that linguistic and religious minorities are covered by the expression 'minority' under Article 30 of the Constitution. Since reorganisation of the States in India has been on linguistic lines, therefore, for the purpose of determining the minority, the unit will be the State and not the whole of India. Thus, religious and linguistic minorities, who have been put at par in Article 30, have to be considered State-wise. In the same case, the Supreme Court has dealt with the concepts of Equality and Secularism and given a clear picture of the implementation mechanism. To quote:

> 'Our country is often depicted as a person in the form of "Bharat Mata Mother India." The people of India are regarded as her children with their welfare being in her heart. Like any loving mother, the welfare of the family is of paramount importance for her. For a healthy family, it is important that each member is strong and healthy. But then, all members do not have the same constitution, whether physical and/or mental. For harmonious and healthy growth, it is but natural for the parents, and the mother in particular, to give more attention and food to the weaker child so as to help him/her become stronger. Giving extra food and attention and ensuring private tuition to help in his/her studies will, in a sense, amount to giving the weaker child preferential treatment. Just as lending physical support to the aged and the infirm, or providing a special diet, cannot be regarded as unfair or unjust, similarly, conferring certain rights on a special class, for good reasons, cannot be considered inequitable. All the people of India are not alike, and that is why preferential treatment to a special section of the society is not frowned upon. Article 30 is a special right conferred on the religious and linguistic minorities because of their numerical handicap and to instill in them a sense of security and confidence, even though the minorities cannot be per se regarded as weaker

sections or underprivileged segments of the society. The one billion population of India consists of six main ethnic groups and fifty-two major tribes; six major religions and 6,400 castes and sub-castes; eighteen major languages and 1,600 minor languages and dialects. The essence of secularism in India can best be depicted if a relief map of India is made in mosaic, where the aforesaid one billion people are the small pieces of marble that go into the making of a map. Each person, whatever his/her language, caste, religion has his/her individual identity, which has to be preserved, so that when pieced together it goes to form a depiction with the different geographical features of India. These small pieces of marble, in the form of human beings, which may individually be dissimilar to each other, when placed together in a systematic manner, produce the beautiful map of India. Each piece, like a citizen of India, plays an important part in making of the whole. The variations of the colours as well as different shades of the same colour in a map is the result of these small pieces of different shades and colours of marble, but even when one small piece of marble is removed, the whole map of India would be scarred, and the beauty would be lost. Each of the people of India has an important place in the formation of the nation. Each piece has to retain its own colour. By itself, it may be an insignificant stone, but when placed in a proper manner, goes into the making of a full picture of India in all its different colours and hues. A citizen of India stands in a similar position. The Constitution recognises the differences among the people of India, but it gives equal importance to each of them, their differences notwithstanding, for only then can there be a unified secular nation. Recognising the need for the preservation and retention of different pieces that go into the making of a whole nation, the Constitution, while maintaining, *inter alia*, the basic principle of equality, contains adequate provisions that

> ensure the preservation of these different pieces. The essence of secularism in India is the recognition and preservation of the different types of people, with diverse languages and different beliefs, and placing them together so as to form a whole and united India. Articles 29 and 30 do not more than seek to preserve the differences that exist, and at the same time, unite the people to form one strong nation."

Religious harmony and national integration, as contemplated in the Constitution, is the need of the hour but religious fanaticism, which is wrongly described as religious fundamentalism, has plagued the global atmosphere. In the Charter of the United Nations, the nations of the world had determined to reaffirm faith in fundamental human rights, in the dignity and worth of the human person and to practice tolerance and live together in peace with one another as good neighbours. But even in the twenty first century, divisive forces and religious fanatics are raising their ugly head. Such elements are bent upon polluting the atmosphere. They are demolishing religious places, desecrating deities, and resorting to loot and arson, besides killing innocent people by applying most inhuman methods. Even women and children are burnt alive.

Communalism is the basic feature of the so called fundamentalism whereas religious harmony and national integration are the basic features of the Indian Constitution. Religion is a deep and moving source of self-identity and, sometimes, it is noticed that group sentiments can be quickly aroused on religious grounds and this noble sentiment is turned into hatred and fanaticism and, as stated above, such communal elements resort to irrational acts. Religious appeal is so appealing that even in 1940 when Stalin was fighting against Hitler's forces and was in trouble decided to appeal to the religious sentiments and religious history of the Soviet people to arouse their patriotic feelings though he was an atheist. Even Saddam Husain who headed a country Constitution of which is/was secular, appealed to the Muslim world to help him in the name of religion. However, it is worth appreciating that in the Indian struggle for freedom people professing different religions participated actively. Those who believed in Two Nation theory and apprehended backlash from opposite quarter migrated to Pakistan and those who believed in One Nation theory and one people, the people of India as also those who reconciled to the changed situation, preferred to stay in India hoping that all of them will be treated as sons of the soil and shall also be treated at par in all walks of life, an expectation yet to be fulfilled, as so confirmed by Sachar Committee and Justice Ranganath Mishra Commission.

The root cause of communalism is the faulty education about other religions and members of other communities. The members of different communities get unbalanced by a communal group label, such as, Hindu, Muslim, Sikh or Christian etc. and tend to think irrationally that only members of their own community are always right or just and others are wrong. In that way, they tilt in favour of their own community and discriminate against members of other communities. It is absolutely an irrational approach.

As a matter of fact, religion is not the root cause of the communal problem but it is the misuse of the religion that leads to it. According to Dr S. Radhakrishnan, religion is a dynamic process, a renewed effort of the creative impulses working through exceptional individuals and seeking to uplift humankind to a new level. But unfortunately what we are noticing today is that we are not uplifting the humankind but we are bringing the humankind to the lowest level by misusing the religion and doing what every religion prohibits to do. In the changed socio-political scenario, the intellectuals have also lost their voice. It is high time that the intellectuals of our country must come forward to undertake the responsibility of creating congenial atmosphere in the country in which all of us may live in peace as brothers and sisters as was expected by the founding fathers of our Constitution. Article 51A of the Constitution provides that it shall be the duty of every citizen of India to abide by the Constitution and respect its ideals and institutions, to cherish and follow the noble ideas which inspired our national struggle for freedom, to uphold and protect the sovereignty, unity and integrity of India, to value and preserve the rich heritage of our composite culture and to develop the scientific temper, humanism and the spirit of enquiry and reform and to strive towards the excellence in all spheres of individual and collective activity so that the nation constantly rises to higher levels of endeavour and achievement. Thus, anyone who does not abide by the Constitution and does not respect its ideals and institutions, strikes at the Constitution itself. It is an act unbecoming of a citizen or national of a civilised country.

The founding fathers of the Constitution were equally worried about the religious harmony in the country. The Constituent Assembly, set-up in view of Cabinet Mission Plan, had also suggested that an Advisory Committee on the rights of the citizens, minorities, tribals and for excluded areas be set up. Thus, the Cabinet Mission Plan itself separately categorised citizens as minorities, tribals and the excluded areas. The Advisory Committee was constituted and its Report was submitted prior to the framing of the Constitution. The framers of the Constitution protected the rights of various minorities throughout the country. In Ahmedabad St. Xavier's College Society v. State of Gujarat (AIR 1974 SC 1389) it was held:-

"There is no mysticism in the secular character of the State. Secularism is neither anti-God nor pro-God. It treats alike the devout, the agnostic and atheist. It eliminates God from the matters of the State and ensures that no one shall be discriminated against on the ground of religion."

Constitutional Provisions for Protection of Minorities

Part-III of the Constitution of India, if acted upon in true letter and spirit, is a complete charter of Human Rights. The provisions contained in this part provide for complete foolproof protective cover to the minorities. Articles reproduced below bear testimony thereto:

Article 14 provides that the State shall not deny to any person equality before law or equal protection of laws within the territory of India. The doctrine of equality before law follows from the concept of the English 'Rule of Law'. Jennings in his book titled '*Law and the Constitution*' has defined the doctrine as under:

"Equality before the means that among equals the law should be equal and should be equally administered that like should be treated alike."

All the articles in Part-III of the Constitution guaranteeing Fundamental Rights and freedoms are, in general, equally applicable to the minorities. However, some of these articles have specially been incorporated for the protection of the minorities.

Article 15 of the Constitution provides that the State shall not discriminate against any citizen on grounds only of religion, race, caste, sex, place of birth or any of them and that no citizen shall, on grounds only of religion, race, caste, sex, place of birth or any of them, be subject to any disability, liability, restriction or condition with regard to excess to shops, public restaurants, hotels and places of public entertainment or the use of wells, tanks, bathing ghats, roads and places of public resort maintained wholly or partly out of State funds or dedicated to the use of general public. But, at the same time, Clauses 3 and 4 of this Article provide that nothing in this article shall prevent the state from making any special provision for women and children and for the advancement of any socially and educationally backward classes of citizens or for the Scheduled Castes and the

Scheduled Tribes. It means that reasonable discrimination which may more rationally be described as reasonable classification is always permissible and this is the reason that the Constitution has incorporated special provisions for the protection of Scheduled Castes, Scheduled Tribes, Socially and educationally backward classes of citizens, minorities and other categories of persons.

Article 16 provides for equality of opportunity in matters of public employment. It reads as under:-

> "(1) There shall be equality of opportunity for all citizens in matters relating to employment or appointment to any office under the State.
>
> (2) No citizen shall, on grounds only of religion, race, caste, sex, descent, place of birth, residence or any of them, be ineligible for, or discriminated against in respect of, any employment or office under the State.
>
> (3) Nothing in this article shall prevent Parliament from making any law prescribing, in regard to a class or classes of employment or appointment to an office (under the Government of, or any local or other authority within, a State or Union Territory, any requirement as to residence within that State or Union Territory) prior to such employment or appointment.
>
> (4) Nothing in this article shall prevent the State from making any provision for the reservation of appointments or posts in favour of any backward class of citizens which, in the opinion of the State, is not adequately represented in the services under the State.

Articles 19 to 22 guarantee various freedoms, such as, protection of certain rights regarding freedom of speech, etc., protection in respect of conviction for offences, protection of life and personal liberty and protection against arrest and detention in certain cases and all these freedoms are available to the minorities in the manner the same are available to the majority community and so is the case of right against exploitation as provided in Articles 23 and 24.

Articles 25 to 28 of the Constitution preserve and protect the freedom of all religions professed in the country.

Article 25 guarantees freedom of conscience and free profession, practice and propagation of religion. It reads as under:-

"(1) Subject to public order, morality and health and to the other provisions of this Part, all persons are equally entitled to freedom of conscience and the right freely to profess, practice and propagate religion.

(2) Nothing in this Article shall affect the operation of any existing law or prevent the State from making any law -

(a) Regulating or restricting any economic, financial, political or other secular activity which may be associated with religious practice;

(b) Providing for social welfare and reform or the throwing open of Hindu religious institutions of a public character to all classes and sections of Hindus.

Explanation 1.—The wearing and carrying of kirpans shall be deemed to be included in the profession of the Sikh religion.

Explanation II.—In sub-clause (b) of Clause (2), the reference to Hindus shall be construed as including a reference to persons professing the Sikh, Jain or Buddhist religion, and the reference to Hindu religious institutions shall be construed accordingly."

A plain reading of the Article indicates that the freedom granted under this Article is subject to certain curbs i.e. subject to public order, morality and health. In other words, the liberty granted under this Article is not unfettered as unfettered liberty may be granted only when the law of jungle is in operation. Such sort of curbs and fetters are required to curb religious fanaticism. It is not only in the Indian Constitution that such a rider has been applied. Even in the most advanced nations of the world and those who claim to be the advocates and champions of human rights and in whose Constitutions it is provided that the religious freedom is an inviolable right, have put such curbs in their Constitutions and rightly so because a civilised society can never permit persons belonging to the majority community or the minority community to resort to religious fanaticism and hurt feelings of each other.

Article 26 grants freedom to manage religious affairs. It reads as under:-

"Subject to public order, morality and health, every religious denomination or any section thereof shall have the right:-

(a) to establish and maintain institutions for religious and charitable purposes;

(b) to manage its own affairs in matters of religion;

(c) to own and acquire movable and immovable property; and

(d) to administer such property in accordance with law."

Article 27 grants freedom as to payment of taxes for promotion of any particular religion. It reads as under:-

"No person shall be compelled to pay any taxes, the proceeds of which are specifically appropriated in payment of expenses for the promotion or maintenance of any particular religion or religious denomination."

Article 28 grants freedom as to attendance at religious instruction or religious worship in certain educational institutions. It reads as under:-

"No religious instruction shall be provided in any educational institution wholly maintained out of State funds.

(2) Nothing in Cl. (1) shall apply to an educational institution which is administered by the State but has been established under any endowment or trust which requires that religious instruction shall be imparted in such institution.

No person attending any educational institution recognised by the State or receiving aid out of State funds shall be required to take part in any religious instruction that may be imparted in such institution or to attend any religious worship that may be conducted in such institution or in any premises attached thereto unless such person or, if such person is a minor, his guardian has given his consent thereto.

29. Protection of interests of minorities.-(1) Any section of the citizens residing in the territory of India or any part thereof having a distinct language, script or culture of its own shall have the right to conserve the same.

(2) No citizen shall be denied admission into any educational institution maintained by the State or receiving aid out of State funds on grounds only of religion, race, caste, language or any of them.

Article 29(2) applies to minorities as well as to non-minorities. When other qualifications being equal the religion, race, caste, language of a citizen shall not be a ground of preference or disability.

30. Right of minorities to establish and administer educational institutions. - (1) All minorities, whether based on religion or language, shall have the right to establish and administer educational institutions of their choice.

(1A) In making any law providing for the compulsory acquisition of any property of an educational institution established and administered by a minority, referred to in clause (1), the State shall ensure that the amount fixed by or determined under such law for the acquisition of such property is such as would not restrict or abrogate the right guaranteed under that clause.

(2) The State shall not, in granting aid to educational institutions, discriminate against any educational institution on the ground that it is under the management of a minority, whether based on religion or language.

Besides Constitution of India various other laws also contain provisions with a bearing on minority rights.

Sections 153A, 153, 295, 295A, 296, 297 and 298 have been included in the Indian Penal Code so that religious feelings of any citizen are not hurt and communal harmony is preserved in its true sense. These sections are reproduced as under:-

"153A. Promoting enmity between different groups of religion, race, place of birth, residence, language, etc., and doing acts prejudicial to maintenance of harmony - (1) -

(a) by words, either spoken or written, or by signs or by visible representations or otherwise, promotes or attempts to promote, on grounds of religion, race, place of birth, residence, language, caste or community or any other ground whatsoever, disharmony or feelings of enmity, hatred, or ill-will between different religious, racial, language or regional groups or castes, or communities; of

(b) commits any act which is prejudicial to the maintenance of harmony between different religious, racial, language or regional groups or castes or communities, and which disturbs or is likely to disturb the public tranquility, or

(c) organises any movement, drill or other similar activity intending that the participants in such activity shall use or be trained to use criminal force or violence or knowing it to be likely that the participants in such activity will use or be trained to use criminal force or violence or participates in such activity intending to use or be trained to use criminal force or violence or knowing it to be likely that the participants, in such activity will use or be trained to use criminal force or violence, against any religious, racial, language or regional group or caste or community and such activity for any reason whatsoever causes or is likely to cause fear or alarm or a feeling of insecurity amongst members of such religious, racial, language or regional group or caste or community,

Shall be punished with imprisonment which may extend to three years, or with fine, or with both.

Offence committed in place of worship etc. - (2) whoever commits an offence specified in sub-section (1) in any place of worship or any assembly engaged in the performance of religious worship or religious ceremonies, shall be punished with imprisonment which may extend to five years and shall also be liable to fine.

153B. Imputations, assertion prejudicial to national integration - (1) whoever, by words either spoken or written or by signs or by visible representations or otherwise, -

(a) makes or publishes any imputation that any class of persons cannot, by reason of their being members of any religious, racial, language or regional group or caste or community, bear true faith and allegiance to the Constitution of India as by law established or uphold the sovereignty and integrity of India, or

(b) asserts, counsels, advises, propagates or publishes that any class of persons shall, by reason of heir being members of any religious, racial, language or regional group or caste or community, be denied or deprived of their rights as citizens of India, or

(c) makes or publishes any assertion, counsel, plea or appeal concerning he obligation of any class of persons, by reason of their being members of any religious, racial, language or regional group or caste or community, and such assertion, counsel, plea or appeal causes or is likely to cause disharmony or feelings of enmity or hatred or ill-will between such members and other persons,

Shall be punished with imprisonment which may extend to three years, or with fine or with both.

(2) Whoever commits an offence specified in sub-section (1) in any place of worship or in any assembly engaged in the performance of religious worship or religious ceremonies, shall be punished with imprisonment which may extend to five years and shall also be liable to fine.

295. Injuring or defiling place of worship with intent to insult the religion of any class - Whoever destroys, damages or defiles any place of worship, or any object held sacred by any class of persons with the intention of thereby insulting the religion of any class of persons or with the knowledge that any class of person is likely to consider such destruction, damage or defilement, as an insult to their religion, shall be punished with imprisonment of either description for a term which may extend to two years, or with fine, or with both.

295A. Deliberate and malicious acts intended to outrage religious feelings of any class by insulting its religion or religious beliefs - Whoever, with deliberate and malicious intention of outraging the religious feelings of any class of citizens of India, by words, either spoken or written or by signs or by visible representations or otherwise insults or attempts to insult the religion or the religious beliefs of that class, shall be punished with imprisonment of either description for a term which may extend to three years or with fine, or with both.

296. Disturbing religious assembly - Whoever voluntarily causes disturbance to any assembly lawfully engaged in the performance of religious worship, or religious ceremonies, shall be punished with imprisonment of either description for a term which may extend to one year, or with fine, or with both.

297. Trespassing on burial places, etc.-Whoever with intention of wounding the feelings of any person or of insulting the religion of any person, or with the knowledge that the feelings of any person are likely to be wounded, or that the religion of any person is likely to be insulted thereby, commits any trespass in any place of worship or on any place of sculpture, or any place set apart for the performance of funeral rites or as a depository for the remains of the dead, or offers any indignity to any human corpse or causes disturbance to any person assembled for the performance of funeral ceremonies, Shall be punished with imprisonment of either description for a term which may extend to one year, or with fine, or with both.

298. Uttering words, etc., with deliberate intent to wound religious feelings - Whoever, with the deliberate intention of wounding the religious feelings of any person, utters any word or makes any sound in the hearing of that person or making any gesture in the sight of that person or places, any object in the sight of that person, shall be punished with imprisonment of either description for a term which may extend to one year, or with fine, or with both."

Thus, the law is perfect but the nation is yet to attain perfection. India has been successfully maintaining its unity from day one of its independence but the growing communal conflict in India may make one feel as if the unity of the country is in jeopardy today. Mistrust amongst various communities is rising and it is to be checked with a firm hand. As regards Muslim community, it is the biggest minority community in India and the way it behaves and is treated, sets the communal temper in our country. There is a section of the society in India which looks upon Muslims still in some way foreign to India. These people forget that they are the sons and daughters of the same soil and the same country. They had made a conscience choice to stay in India in 1947. They preferred secular state to an Islamic State. They are to be rewarded for it and not punished. It will not be wrong to say that majority of the Indian Muslims of partitioned India were also secular as most of them preferred to stay in India. Another important factor which many of us are ignoring in the changed scenario is that the Muslim clergy was by and large more secular than those who had received western education. It is common knowledge that Dar-ul-Uloom, Deoband had whole-heartedly supported freedom movement. With this background, there is no cogent reason for treating Indian Muslims as second rate citizens, may be by a section of the people. Bharat Mata which they (Indian Muslims) call mather-I-Hind is as sacred to them as it is to the majority community or any other minority community. Communal harmony cannot be achieved by fighting or finding fault with each other or criticising each other's religions. It can be achieved only through positive cooperation of all communities and sincere efforts by the State. Good and bad are not to be treated at par. There should be an objective exercise to separate chaff from the grain so that innocent people are not penalised and they are not subject to any inhuman and derogatory treatment and furthermore their human rights that are enshrined in the International covenants and the Constitution of India are not violated.

At the same time, it is also equally important that all minorities whether Muslims, Christians, Sikhs or Parsis must not do anything that hurts the feelings of the majority community. Communal harmony is a reciprocal concept. Do good to others, only then they will do good to you. It is the constitutional duty of the minority communities to conduct themselves in such a manner that they earn the trust and confidence of the majority community. They must realise that the religious feelings of the majority community are as sacred to them as their feelings are to them. They cannot bulldoze the majority community by their irresponsible behaviour.*

* An extract from the author's book titled '*Hindu-Muslim Unity and Love for India*' published by Gyan Publishing House, New Delhi.

CHAPTER 8

Had Maulana been alive to watch the present day situation of Muslims live and fix the responsibility?

Present day plight of Indian Muslims as per Government record and as per Sachar Committee Report is as under:

Salient Findings of the Sachar Committee

(i) Education:

(a) The literacy rate among Muslims was 59.1 per cent, which was below the national average of 64.8 per cent.

(b) The mean years of schooling (MYS) is lower compared to the average MYS for all children.

(c) 25 per cent of Muslim children in the age of 6 – 14 year age group have either never attended school or have dropped out.

(d) The majority of Muslim girls and boys fail in their matriculation examination or drop out before that.

(e) Less than 4 per cent of Muslims are graduates or diploma holders compared to about 7 per cent of the population aged 20 years and above.

(f) There is a strong desire and enthusiasm for education among Muslim women and girls across the board.

(g) Schools beyond primary level are few in Muslim localities.

Exclusive schools for girls are fewer.

(h) Lack of hostel facilities is a limiting factor, especially for girls.

(i) Muslim parents are not averse to modern or mainstream education and to sending their children to affordable

Government schools. They do not necessarily prefer to send children to madarsas. However, the access to government schools for Muslim children is limited.

(ii) Skill development

(a) Skill development initiatives for those who have not completed school education may be particularly relevant for some sections of Muslims given their occupational structure.

(b) The skill demands in the manufacturing and service sectors are changing continuously and youth with middle school education would meet these needs.

(c) A rehabilitation package for innovative re-skilling and for upgrading the occupational structure in the wake of liberalisation is seen as an urgent need.

(iii) Employment and economic opportunities:

(a) Self-employment is the main source of income of Muslims. They are engaged more in self-employed manufacturing and trade activities compared to others.

(b) The share of Muslim workers engaged in street vending is the highest. More than 12 per cent of Muslim male workers are engaged in street vending as compared to the national average of less than 8 per cent.

(c) The percentage of women Muslim workers undertaking work within their own homes is much larger at 70 per cent compared to all workers at 51 per cent.

(d) The share of Muslims in the total workers engaged in the tobacco and textiles/garment related industries are quite significant.

(e) The share of Muslim workers in production related activities and transport equipment operation is much higher at 34 per cent, as against 21 per cent of all workers.

More than 16 per cent of Muslims were engaged as sales workers, while the national average was only about 10 per cent.

While the participation of Muslim workers is relatively higher in production and sales related occupations, their participation was relatively lower in professional, technical, clerical and to some extent managerial work.

Muslims, by and large, are engaged in the unorganised sector of the economy and have to bear the brunt of liberalisation. The participation of Muslims in regular salaried jobs is much less than workers of other socio-religious categories.

(j) Muslims are relatively more vulnerable in terms of conditions of work as their concentration in informal sector employment is higher and their job conditions, even among regular workers, are less for Muslims than those of other socio-religious communities.

(k) Percentage of households availing banking facilities is much lower in villages where the share of Muslim population is high.

(iv) Poverty and development

(a) About 38 per cent of Muslims in urban areas and 27 per cent in rural areas live below the poverty level.

(b) Muslims are concentrated in locations with poor infrastructure facilities. This affects their access to basic services like education, health facilities, transport, etc.

(c) About a third of small villages with high concentration of Muslims do not have any educational institutions.

(d) There is a scarcity of medical facilities in larger villages with a substantial Muslim concentration. About 40 per cent of large villages with a substantial Muslim concentration do not have any medical facilities.

(e) Muslim concentration villages are not well served with pucca roads.

(f) Policies to deal with the relative deprivation of the Muslims in the country should sharply focus on inclusive development and mainstreaming of the community while respecting diversity.

(v) Social conditions

(a) A community-specific factor for low educational achievement is that Muslims do not see education as necessarily translating into formal employment.

(b) The Muslim population shows an increasingly better sex ratio compared with other socio-religious communities.

(c) Infant and childhood mortality among Muslims is slightly lower than the average.

(d) There has been a large decline in fertility in all the religious groups including Muslims.

Recommendation-wise follow up action on Sachar Committee Report as provided by Ministry of Minority Affairs, Government of India

I. Educational Empowerment

Government is giving special emphasis on free and compulsory school education to the age of 14. The emphasis is on to (i) create educational infrastructure for easy accessibility to the children in the areas with substantial minority population minority concentration and (ii) to promote education through various other means such as scholarships to needy children, promotion of education among minority girl children, quality education through Madarsas and Maktabs, etc. A coordinated effort in this direction is being made through Ministry of Human Resource Development.

The Department of School Education and Literacy has launched Sakshar Bharat the new variant of the National Literacy Mission on 08.09.2009 for implementation in the 11th Plan with an objective to make 70 million non-literate adults literates by the end of the Plan. The Scheme has special focus on women belonging to minorities.

The Mid-day meal scheme was extended to all areas in the country from the year 2007-08 onwards and also covers upper primary schools. Blocks with concentration of Muslim population are covered under this scheme. Children in Madarsas are also covered under the programme. Planning Commission has approved the extension of the scheme to students studying in privately managed unaided schools located in SC, ST and Minority Concentrated Districts. Benefitting approximately 60.37 lakh children in 29116 schools in MCDs and special focused districts.

Sarva Shiksha Abhiyan (SSA) is being implemented and a considerable educational infrastructure such as primary schools, upper primary schools have been opened/ constructed. SSA is committed to ensuring universal access to primary and upper primary education within one km and three kms respectively. States have been advised to give primacy to opening of Girls only Upper Primary Schools.

Under SSA the following works have been taken up since 2006-07 in the minority concentration districts:

Primary schools constructed: 15765

Upper primary school constructed: 8131

Additional classrooms constructed: 230581

New primary schools opened: 17870

Upper primary schools opened: 11857

No of teachers sanctioned: 125375

555 Kasturba Gandhi Balika Vidyalayas have been sanctioned since 2006-07.

The Ministry of Minority Affairs is implementing three Scholarship schemes namely, Pre-matric, Post-matric and Merit-cum-means based scholarship schemes for the students of minority communities. The details of scholarships given till 31.01.2014 are as under:

Pre-matric Scholarship: 260 lakh

Post-matric Scholarship: 32.26 lakh

Merit-cum-means Scholarship: 3.14 lakh

Total scholarships given: 295.40 lakh -.

30 per cent of scholarships are earmarked for girls.

All the State Governments/Union Territory Administrations have been advised by the Ministry of HRD for using existing school buildings and community buildings as the study centres for school children. Reminders have been periodically issued to the Chief Secretaries of all states/ UTs in this regard.

M/o HRD (Department of School Education and Literacy) has also issued instructions that as KGBV schools are part of the regular upper primary school system of the State, the State Government / Union Territory. Particular policy for instruction in Urdu medium should be adopted for the KGBV schools. The Urdu teachers available in the system should be deployed for the purpose. Continued efforts have been made by M/o HRD to increase enrollment of Muslim girls in these KGBVs.

In order to increase enrollment of girls belonging to minority communities, States have been requested in July 2013 to take immediate steps to enroll the most vulnerable/drop-out girls from the minority communities in the KGBVs so as to enhance their opportunities.

2. Provision of hostel facilities

UGC has sanctioned 285 Women's Hostels during 11th Plan in 90 Minority Concentration Districts. During 2012-13, out of 148 women's hostels, 25 have been sanctioned in minority concentration districts.

During 2013-14 (up to 30.09.2013), 68 Women's Hostels have been approved/sanctioned in MCDs.

3. Teachers' training to include sensitisation towards the needs and aspirations of Muslims and other marginalised communities.

The Centrally Sponsored Scheme in the XII Plan *inter-alia* envisages establishment of Block Institutes of Teachers Education in 196 SC/ST/Minority Concentration Districts (MCDs). This has covered 15 States/ UTs. Up to August 2013, 96 BITEs have been sanctioned.

The Department of School Education and Literacy has launched Sakshar Bharat the new variant of the National Literacy Mission on 08.09.2009 for implementation in the 11th Plan with an objective to make 70 million non-literate adults literates by the end of the Plan. The Scheme has special focus on women belonging to minorities. Sakshar Bharat is being implemented in

372 districts out of the 410 eligible districts where adult female literacy rate is 50 per cent or below as per 2001 census. 66 MCDs have been covered under this programme.

Jan Shikshan Sansthans (JSSs) are imparting vocational training in 33 out of the 88 Muslim dominated districts in the country. Action for covering additional districts with substantial minority population is under process. A proposal for opening 55 JSSs in MCDs is under consideration.The coverage under this programme during 2012-13 was 12.2 per cent. In the year 2013-14 (upto October, 2013) out of 248757 beneficiaries, 30,629 (12.31 per cent) belong to minorities. The coverage is commensurate with the percentage of minority population in the districts where these JSSs are functioning.

All the State Governments/Union Territory Administrations have been advised by the Ministry of HRD for using existing school buildings and community buildings as the study centres for school children. Reminders have been periodically issued to the Chief Secretaries of all states/ UTs in this regard.

Under the Scheme for Providing Quality Education in Madarsa (SPQEM), the objective is to encourage traditional institutions like Madarsas and Maktabs by giving financial assistance to introduce science, mathematics, social studies, hindi and english in their curriculum so that academic proficiency for classes 1-XII is attainable for children studying in these institutions.

Similarly, the scheme for Infrastructure Development of Minority Institutions (IDMI) would facilitate education of minorities by augmenting and strengthening school infrastructure in Minority Institutions (elementary/ secondary/senior secondary schools) in order to expand facilities for formal education to children of minority communities. The scheme will *inter alia* encourage educational facilities for girls, children with special needs and those who are most deprived educationally amongst minorities.

4. Recognition of the degree from Madarsas for eligibility in competitive examination e.g. Civil Services, Banks, Defence services etc. Equivalence to Madarsas certification/degrees for admission to higher education institutions be given.

The certificates / qualifications of the Madrasa Boards which have been granted equivalence by the State Education Board to that of their Secondary and Senior Secondary qualification have been equated with corresponding certificates of the Central Board of Secondary Education (CBSE), Council of Board of School Education in India (COBSE) and other school examination boards, for the purpose of employment and entry to higher levels education. DOPT has issued notification in this connection.

5. Recognition of minority educational institutions

With respect to Mechanism for granting of Minority Educational Institution status more responsive, National Commission for Minority Educational Institutions (NCMEI) has been established by an Act of Parliament with the key objective of ensuring that the true amplitude of the educational rights enshrined in Article 30 (1) of the Constitution is made available to the members of the notified religious minority communities, including the Muslims.

M/O HRD has informed that from 2005 to June, 2013, 8261 certificates have been issued for granting minority educational institute.

M/o HRD has informed that action has been initiated to develop data in respect of enrolment of the minorities in higher educational institutions.

6. Scheme for modernisation of Madarsas

The Area Intensive and Madarsa Modernisation Programme has been recast as two schemes, namely, the Scheme of Providing Quality Education in Madarsas (SPQEM). and Scheme for Infrastructure Development Private Aided/Unaided Minority Institutes (Elementary / Secondary / Senior Secondary Schools). The scheme is demand driven.

12,739 Madarsas and 30,507 teachers assisted under SPQEM with an amount of Rs 283.53 crores during 11th Five Year Plan (FYP). In the 12th Plan, during 2012-13, 9,905 Madarsas and 23,146 teachers assisted under SPQEM with total sanctioned amount of Rs.182.49 crores. During 2013-14 (upo September, 2013), 4,553 Madarsas and 12,229 teachers assisted with total sanctioned amount of Rs 58.01 crores.

Under IDMI, total 405 minority institutions assisted and Rs 75.89 crores released during 11th Five Year Plan (FYP). In the 12th Plan, during 2012-13, 184 minority institutions assisted and Rs 128.38 crores released. During 2013-14 (upto Sept., 2013), 81 minority institutions assisted and Rs 11.26 crores released.

7. Increase in the Corpus of Maulana Azad Education Foundation

The corpus of MAEF was increased from Rs 200 crore to Rs 750 crore during the 11th Plan. The present corpus is of the order of Rs 910 crore and the same has been approved to be raised to Rs 1250 crore by the end of 12th Plan.

8. Evaluation of the content of the school text books

16 States {Andhra Pradesh, Bihar, Chhattisgarh, Haryana (Pr), Karnataka, Kerala, Manipur, Mizoram, Meghalaya, Nagaland, Odisha, Uttar Pradesh, Uttarakhand, Gujarat, Madhya Pradesh and Tamil Nadu} have completed revising their

curriculum in the light of NCF 2005, while 5 States (Assam, Himachal Pradesh, Maharashtra, Sikkim and Tripura) are currently in the process of doing so, and 11 States/UTs (Chandigarh, Delhi, Goa, Haryana, Himachal Pradesh, Jammu & Kashmir, Jharkhand, Lakshadweep, Rajasthan, Arunachal Pradesh and Andaman & Nicobar Islands} follow the NCERT syllabus. 3UTs {Daman & Diu, Dadra & Nagar Haveli and Puducherry) have followed the curriculum of neighbouring States.

MHRD has informed that based on the recommendations of National curriculum 2005, NCERT revised the syllabi and prepared new textbooks of all the subjects for all stages of school education. The whole exercise of revision of syllabus and textbooks supervised by the National Monitoring Committee appointed by the Department of Secondary and Higher Education. The textbook of secondary and higher secondary stages for geography, political science, economics, sociology, commerce, physics, chemistry, biology and Mathematics have been reviewed and updated. The syllabus has been revised by almost all the State Govt. either by revision, or by adopting the syllabus of neighbouring States.

9. Access to Credit

Under the Scheme Priority Sector Lending being implemented by Department of Financial Services, lending to minority communities is covered under weaker sections category of Priority Sector Lending. RBI has issued its Master circular on 1st July, 2013 on priority sector lending for improving credit facilities to minority communities.

The percentage of Priority Sector Lending (PSL) going to minorities has shown steady increase from 10.6 per cent in 2007-08, 12.24 per cent in 2008-09, 13.01 per cent in 2009-10, 14.16 per cent in 2010-11, 14.55 per cent in 2011-12, 14.59 per cent in 2012-13 and 14.93 per cent in September 2013. The segregated community-wise details of

PSL for the year 2013-14 upto September, 2013 are given below:

Muslims : 47.01 per cent

Christians : 21.58 per cent

Sikhs : 27.49 per cent

Buddhists : 2.15 per cent

Parsis : 1.77 per cent

A total of 18,043 branches have been opened in areas with substantial minority population upto September, 2013.

Entrepreneurial Development Programme

Steps to be introduced to direct credit to Muslims, create awareness of various credit schemes through publicity, Entrepreneurial development programmes.

RBI has instructed the lead banks to organise entrepreneur development programmes so that members of the minority communities in these areas could derive the benefits of various programmes being financed by the banks.

Department of Financial Services has informed that 2189 entrepreneur development programmes (EDPs) have been organised during 2013-14 (upto September 2013) and the number of beneficiaries is 27,543 while the amount of financial assistance provided was Rs 64.40 crore to 17365 beneficiaries.

As per the information provided by the Department of Financial Services, 3,848,478 accounts have been opened for minority women with Rs 23,402.83 crore as Micro-credit to them upto September, 2013.

One of the components under the Revamped Scheme of Swarna Jayanti Shahari Rozgar Yojana (SJSRY) is the Urban

Women Self-Help Programme (UWSP). This programme focuses on assisting groups of urban poor women in setting up of group enterprises with bank loan and subsidy under the scheme. UWSP also assists women groups with revolving funds for thrift and credit activities. Advisory has been issued by Ministry of Housing and Urban Poverty Alleviation to State Governments to take action for promotion of micro-finance among minority women under UWSP component of SJSRY in minority concentration clusters/ towns/ cities.

603 no. of minority beneficiaries covered through group micro enterprises under UWSP. Community-wise segregated data for minority communities (achievement percentage of the respective minority community w.r.t. total achievement for minorities) is as under:

(a) Muslims: 93.04
(b) Sikhs: 0.17
(c) Christians: 4.63
(d) Buddhists: 2.16
(e) Parsis: 22,715 no. of minority beneficiaries covered under revolving fund for T & CS under UWSP.

Community-wise segregated data for minority communities (achievement percentage of the respective minority community w.r.t. total achievement for minorities) is as under:

(a) Muslims: 85.81
(b) Sikhs: 0.02
(c) Christians: 14.10
(d) Buddhists: 0.07

A proposal for restructuring of NMDFC is underway in consultation with merchant banker, namely, SBI-CAPS, and various Ministries, departments concerned.

10. Skill Development and Economics Empowerment

Report of Inter-Ministerial Task Force headed by Dr BL Mungekar was examined. 338 towns/cities having a substantial minority population, of which 251 are backward, have been identified. The following were the broad recommendations:

(1) The identified deficiencies in educational and health infrastructure are to be attended on priority by Deptt. of School Education and Literacy, Deptt. of Higher Education, Ministry of Women and Child Development, Ministry of Labour and Employment and Ministry of Health and Family Welfare.

(2) The identified deficiencies in basic civic amenities are to be attended on priority by Ministry of Urban Development (JNNURM) and Ministry of Housing and Urban Poverty Alleviation (BSUP) and (IHSDP).

(3) Percentage of priority sector lending to minorities to be stepped up to 15 per cent by 2010 by the Deptt. of Financial Services.

Ministries/Departments concerned have been suitably advised.

A three-tier institutional structure for skill development was functioning till May, 2013 at the Central level involving the Prime Minister's National Council on Skill Development (PMNCSD), National Skill Development Co-Ordination Board (NSDCB) under the Planning Commission and the National Skill Development Corporation (NSDC). However, as per a decision of the Union Cabinet the PMNCSD, NSDCB and O/o Adviser to PM on Skill Development has been subsumed in the National Skill Development Agency (NSDA). The NSDA is an autonomous body under the M/o Finance and has been set up *inter alia*, to coordinate and harmonise the skill development efforts of the Government and the Private Sector to achieve the skilling targets of the 12th Plan and beyond and endeavour to bridge the Social, Regional, Gender and Economic Divide.

Pursuant to a Cabinet decision, Cabinet Committee on Skill Development (CCSD) has also been set up *inter alia*, to provide directions and consider all Policies, Programmes, Schemes and initiatives for Skill Development aimed at increasing the employability of the workforce for effectively meeting the emerging requirements of the rapidly growing economy and mapping the benefits of Demographic Dividend. The NSDC will continue to function as a not for profit company under the M/o Finance for fostering private sector initiatives on Skill Development in the country as well as other functions including setting up of Sector Skill Councils (SSCs) and undertaking skill gap studies.

The Ministry of Labour and Employment has informed that 1453 out of 9404 ITIs/ITCs (15.45 per cent) affiliated to NCVT are in Minority Concentration Areas with a capacity of 2,28,840 seats.

Ministry of Minority Affairs has launched a specific scheme “Seekho Aur Kamao” for the skill training of the minority youth. Also, for the creation of infrastructure for skill training in minority concentration areas, 116 ITIs and 44 polytechniques have been approved under Multi-sectoral Development Programme (MsDP). Further, MsDP has earmarked 10 per cent of the total allocation for the skill training of mining youth.

The entry qualification for admission to ITIs be reduced to Class VIII.

The entry qualifications for various trades under Craftsmen Scheme (CTS) implemented through ITIs / ITCs are prescribed as per knowledge and skill requirement to understand course content of the trade. These are decided as per recommendations of trade and committees constituted for each trade, comprising of experts in the field, both from industry and academics. At Present, 19 trades are for students having VIIIth class pass qualification.

10. Special Development Initiatives

Multi-sectoral Development Programme (MsDP) was launched in 90 identified minority concentration districts (MCD) in 2008-09.

The Cabinet Committee on Economic Affairs (CCEA) has approved the restructuring of Multi-sectoral Development Programme on 04.06.2013 for implementation in 710 blocks and 66 towns during the 12th Five Year Plan.

Plans for Rs 6020.15 crore have been approved and Rs 4318.99 crore released to State Governments and UTs up to 30.11.2013 since launching of the programme.

11. Provision of all basic amenities, good quality schools, health facilities, general improvement in living conditions, electricity/housing/clean drinking water in all villages/towns/habitations.

This has been implemented through the schemes of Ministry of Urban Development and Ministry of Housing and Urban Poverty Alleviation (HUPA) and Ministry of Drinking Water and Sanitation through their various schemes. M/o HUPA which have issued advisory to ensure that under the JNNURM / UIDSSMT Schemes, the Detailed Project Reports (DPRs) should have adequate provision for minorities.

Achievements under these schemes are as below:

Under Integrated Housing and Slum Development Programme (IHSDP), at the end of the year 2012-13, out of the total project cost of Rs 11877.30 crore covering 919 cities/towns, Rs 2241.41 crore (18.87 per cent) was sanctioned for 234 cities/towns

(11.21 per cent) having substantial minority population. Out of total 1082 projects approved under this programme, 144 projects (13.3 per cent) are for the towns with substantial minority population. Out of total 558974 dwelling units approved under this programme, 94159 dwelling units (16.84 per cent) are for the towns with substantial minority population.

Under Basic Services to Urban Poor (BSUP), at the end of the year 2012-13, out of the total project cost of Rs 29770.39 crore covering 65 cities/towns, Rs 7254.84 crore (24.36 per cent) was sanctioned for 17 cities/towns (26.15 per cent) having substantial minority population. Out of total 525 projects approved under this programme, 110 projects (21 per cent) are for the towns with substantial minority population. Out of total 1003754 dwelling units approved under this programme, 200527 dwelling units (20 per cent) are for the towns with substantial minority population.

Under Urban Infrastructure Development Scheme for Small and Medium Towns (UIDSSMT), as on 30.06.2013, out of total projects sanctioned at a cost of Rs 14995.58 crores for 718 towns/ cities, projects costing Rs 2725.24 crore (18.17 per cent) are for 88 minority concentration towns/ cities (12.25 per cent). As on 30.06.2013, out of 856 no. of total projects approved, 110 projects (12.85 per cent) are for minority concentration towns/ cities.

Under Urban Infrastructure and Governance (UIG), as on 30.06.2013, out of total projects sanctioned at a cost of Rs 62116.67 crores for 65 towns/cities, projects costing Rs 9476.71 crore are for 17 minority concentration towns/ cities. As on 30.06.2013, out of 563 no. of total projects approved, 77 projects (13.67 per cent) are for minority concentration towns/ cities.

Under National Rural Drinking Water Programme (NRDWP), 21.12 per cent of the funds flow to the areas with substantial minority population.

V. Wakfs

The registration of Trusts set up by Muslim communities such as Wakf and Mosque committees be facilitated.

For the purpose of sensitisation, Department of Personnel and Training has already taken action in this regard and State Government / UT administration have been given modules for training.

Besides, during 11th Plan, UGC has released Rs 46.07 crore for establishment of 2328 Centres of Equal Opportunity (CEOs) in 23 Central Universities, 114 State Universities and 12 Deemed Universities.

12. Better utilisation of Wakf properties

A Public Sector Undertaking namely, National Wakf Development Corporation (NAWADCO) has been incorporated by MoMA in January, 2014 with an authorised share capital of Rs 500 crores and paid up capital of Rs 100 crore, to finance the development of Waqf properties for public purposes throughout the country.

Amendment of Wakf Act, 1995 has been amended by the Wakf (Amendment) Act, 2013 for better management of Waqf properties and their speedy evacuation from illegal occupants.

13. Centres of Equal Opportunity

During 11th Plan, UGC has released Rs 46.07 crore for establishment of 2328 Centres of Equal Opportunity (CEOs) in 23 Central Universities, 114 State Universities and 12 Deemed Universities.

14. Creation of a National Data Bank (NDB) and

15. DoPT's instructions to Ministries of HRD, Home Affairs and Health and Family Welfare for issuing necessary guidelines

regarding posting of Muslim police personnel in thanas and Muslim health personnel and teachers in Muslim concentration areas.

Department of Personnel and Training (DoPT) has issued instructions to Ministries of HRD, Home Affairs and Health and Family Welfare for issuing necessary guidelines regarding posting of Muslim police personnel in thanas and Muslim health personnel and teachers in Muslim concentration areas. In response, suitable circulars have been issued by MHA, Ministry of Health and Ministry of Family Welfare and M/o HRD in this regard.

VII. Miscellaneous

1. Minority representations in Local Bodies to be enhanced

Action taken for Urban Local Bodies:

Ministry of Urban Development has informed that the following States/UTs have taken action for improving the representation of minorities in local bodies- Andhra Pradesh, Chandigarh, Daman & Diu, Haryana, Karnataka, Kerala, Lakshadweep, Odisha, Tamil Nadu and West Bengal. Arunachal Pradesh has not constituted Urban Local Bodies (ULB) so far. The Government of Chhattisgarh is considering the matter. In Himachal Pradesh there is no provision in HP Municipal Acts for representation of minorities in ULB.

Action taken for Rural Local Bodies:

M/o Panchyati Raj has issued requisite advisory letter to all the State Govts. for improving representation of minorities in local bodies on the lines of the initiative taken by the Andhra Pradesh government.

Transparent recruitment system to be provided by inclusion of minorities in the Selection Committee/Boards.

DOPT has issued instructions to all Ministries /Departments and state governments for ensuring representation of minority community in Selection Committee/Board for making recruitment to 10 or more vacancies in group, C & D posts/services. The instructions have also been forwarded to UPSC as majority of group A & B recruitments are made through UPSC.

The Prime Minister's 15 Point provides *inter-alia* for earmarking 15 per cent of the target/outlays for minorities in various important flagship programmes of Ministries/ Departments. There are 17 schemes of 10 Ministries/Departments apart from seven schemes of the M/o Minority Affairs included in the programme. There is a proposal to expand the basket of schemes to cover more programmes under PM.s 15PP.

A transparent recruitment process in the areas of Muslim concentration

Deptt. of Personnel and Training has issued necessary guidelines through Office Memorandum dated 08.01.2007. DoPT has also issued instructions vide letter number 39016/2(s)/ 2009-Estt.(B) dated 17.09.2011 to all appointing authorities to scrupulously observe the following guidelines:

(i) The composition of Selection Committees should be representative. It should be mandatory to have one member belonging to Scheduled Caste (SC)/ Scheduled Tribes (ST) and one member belonging to minority community in Selection Boards/Communities for making recruitment to 10 or more vacancies.

(ii) Where the number of vacancies against which selection is to be made is less than 10, efforts should be made to have the Scheduled Caste/Tribes officer and a Minority community officer included in such Communities/Boards.

(iii) Wide publicity should be given to all appointments in government, public sector banks and financial institutions.

Advertisements should be issued in the language(s) spoken by large number of people of the State / Union Territories, apart from English and Hindi. Further, for Group C level posts, having only basic qualifying requirements, information about vacancies for recruitment should also be disseminated through schools and colleges in that area, in addition to normal channels.

(iv) Where there is concentration of minority community population in local areas, the vacancy circular in local language may be distributed in those areas by suitable arrangements.

Wakf properties be exempted from Rent Control Act

The following States/UTs have exempted Wakf Properties from the purview of RCA - Andhra Pradesh, Bihar, Chhattisgarh, Karnataka, Kerala, Jharkhand, Madhya Pradesh, Punjab, Rajasthan, Uttar Pradesh, Chandigarh, Lakhsadweep and Puducherry. As intimated by Arunachal Pradesh, Nagaland and Daman & Diu, they have no Wakf Properties. The following States do not have RCA- Manipur, Odisha and Andaman Nicobar Islands. The RCAs in the following States are under consideration- Assam, Gujarat, Haryana, Himachal Pradesh, Goa, Meghalaya and West Bengal.

Thus, 10 States and three UTs have amended their respective rent control acts for exemption of Waqf properties. Further seven States have indicated that the matter is under examination while three States and two UTs have clarified that there are no rent control acts. two States have confirmed that no Waqf property exists.

Muslims being engaged in petty mechanical and technical work may also derive maximum advantage from massive Skill India Mission recently launched by the prime minister provided they are provided easy and equitable access to such a mission and the NGOs help them in the process. Above all they also come forward to avail the opportunity. They lack initiative and are afraid of paper work involved in the process. Angels would not come from heaven to help them. They must realise that self help is the best help. However, sometimes helping hand, be it of the state or members of the civil society becomes inevitable. Let the state, bureaucracy and the civil society must play a positive, constructive and result-oriented role failing which entire exercise may prove to be an exercise in futility.

Maulana's Presumptive Reaction

Even after an eye bird view of Sachar Committee Report he would have heaved a sigh of grief and recollected the assurance he had given to Indian Muslims at the pulpit of Jama Masjid, Delhi that they will be getting another lease of life in the changed scenario, of course, not a miserable life. He would have commented 'My fellow freedom fighters and the then rulers and custodian of democracy did not do what they ought to have done for uplifting Muslim Community and further said 'they did not practice whatever they had preached'.

But after having gone through the details of follow up action on Sachar Committee Report as provided by Ministry of Minority Affairs, Government of India, he would have put the following questions to the state (centre and states) and the people.

Maulana's questions to the centre and states

When the schemes are so attractive why the Muslims are so backward economically, socially as also politically ?

Why they are living in slum areas?

Why sanitary conditions and medical facilities are so poor in these areas?

Why they are educationally so poor even after more than six decades of India's independence?

Why their representation is so poor in the central as also state services?

Are they not available even for the posts of peons, drivers and mechanics and other class IV services?

Why the states are taking undue advantage of the federal system which we had provided to them for the good of the people and not for refraining from implementation of minority friendly schemes and legislation?

Ultimately he would have said 'I am not making any political statement or criticising any political party-I am simply telling those being at the helms of the affairs throughout that they did not discharge their duties as honestly and religiously as they ought to have discharged'.

Maulana's questions to the Muslim Community

Why have you been so lethargic in availing of government facilities?

You complain of non-implementation of schemes by biased state personnel, you may be correct to some extent but what NGOs and leaders championing your cause have been doing so far? Have they helped or rendered any assistance to you in completing the formalities for availing of these facilities?

How many educational institutions have been established by you? What action have you taken to remove illiteracy and eradication of poverty?

What action have you taken to make religious education as employment oriented? How many madrasas are giving modern employment oriented education without government help?

Is there any theological or religious bar to imparting modern education in such institutions? Is it not a viable proposition to improve the lot of the students and inculcate the spirit of scientific temperament to make them better citizens?

Have you given prescribed amount of *Zakat* to the poor and managed Waqf properties honestly?

Have your own people not grabbed large number of Waqf properties? Have you or at least some of you not colluded with the encroachers of Waqf properties through underhand transactions?

He would have advised Indian Muslims as under:

"Mere holding seminars, raising slogans and criticising the state will not yield fruitful results. You have to act upon. You have to come forward. Your approach should be pragmatic. Don't loose heart even in compelling situation(s). No one will stop you. Find a way or make one. This country is yours, you belong to it and any fundamental decisions about its destiny will remain incomplete without your consent. But you have to display utmost tolerance and patience even in provocative situation(s). Anger is able to destroy lives and relationships and Prophet Muhammad called it a hot coal on the heart of a descendant of Adam.[[1] At Tirmidhi] The Prophet said, "If anyone suppresses anger when he is in a position to give vent to it, God, the exalted, will call him on the Day of Resurrection and ask him to choose from the rewards offered."[[2] Abu Dawood] He also said, "No one has swallowed back anything more excellent in the sight of God, who is Great and Glorious, than anger, seeking to please God."[[3] At Tirmidhi]. Once a man came to Prophet Mohammad and said, "Messenger of God, teach me some words which I can live by. Do not make them too much for me, in case I forget." He said, "Do not be angry."[[4] Saheeh Al-Bukhari]. The Prophet also advised: "Anger comes from Satan, Satan was created from fire, and fire is extinguished only with water; so when any of you is angry, he should perform ablution."[Abu Dawood]. Once Prophet Muhammad said to his companions, "I know words that if he were to say then his anger would go away, if he said, "I seek refuge with Allah from Satan," what he feels would go away."[Saheeh Al-Bukhari]

According to Imam Ahmad bin Hunbal, Prophet Muhammad had also advised that "If any of you becomes angry, let him keep silent." If a person is trying to be silent, it will obviously restrict his ability to fight or utter obscenities and harsh words. The Quran defines righteous people as, "Those who spend (in God's Cause) in prosperity and in adversity, who repress anger, and who pardon the people; verily, God loves the good-doers." (Quran 3:134).

Always behave as good citizens. This approach may be reformative even for those who do not behave as such. Time is always short, art is always long, so one has to press on. Yet you have miles and miles to go. You can reach desired heights only through your dynamism and positive approach and not through mere lamentation and chanting or reciting a '*marsiya*' an elegiac poem written to commemorate the martydom and valour of Hussain Ibn-i-Ali and his comrades in 'Karbala' every now and then. Every day is not the day of mourning. If you feel that there is a vicious circle around you, try to come out of it. For an optimist, every day is a good day."

CHAPTER 9

Maulana Azad as a Champion of Human Rights

Maulana Azad was championing the cause of human rights at a time when, what to talk of municipal and global legislation on the subject, even the Universal Declaration of Human Rights was yet to come on record.

Fight Against Injustice

Maulana fully realised right from the day he attained age of discretion (the age when one can distinguish between good and bad) that the feeling of injustice rankled human heart most. Justice Brennan of the US had also made an observation in a judicial verdict after several decades. To quote:

"Nothing rankles more in the human heart than a brooding sense of injustice. Illness we can put up with. But injustice makes us want to pull things down. When only the rich can enjoy the law, as a doubtful luxury, and the poor, who need it most, cannot have it because its expense puts it beyond their reach, the threat to the continued existence of free democracy is not imaginary but very real, because democracy's very life depends upon making the machinery of justice so effective that every citizen shall believe in and benefit by its impartiality and fairness."

Maulana Azad has always been conveying to the people, the message of equality, liberty, human dignity, justice to all, freedom from slavery and foreign rule, unity among different communities, brotherhood, no cruel treatment against anyone etc. His speeches and articles covering a period of more than half century are the documentary evidence that whatever he preached, he practiced that, too. We can lay our hands on some of the articles of Universal Declaration of Human Rights, 1948 containing the values that Maulana cherished and expressed in his speeches, of course, not in the language of a legislative draftsman.

Article 1

All human beings are born free and equal in dignity and rights. They are endowed with reason and conscience and should act towards one another in a spirit of brotherhood.

Article 2

Everyone is entitled to all the rights and freedoms set forth in this Declaration, without distinction of any kind, such as race, colour, sex, language, religion, political or other opinion, national or social origin, property, birth or other status. Furthermore, no distinction shall be made on the basis of the political, jurisdictional or international status of the country or territory to which a person belongs, whether it be independent, trust, non-self-governing or under any other limitation of sovereignty.

Article 3

Everyone has the right to life, liberty and security of person.

Article 4

No one shall be held in slavery or servitude; slavery and the slave trade shall be prohibited in all their forms.

Article 5

No one shall be subjected to torture or to cruel, inhuman or degrading treatment or punishment.

Article 7

All are equal before the law and are entitled without any discrimination to equal protection of the law. All are entitled to equal protection against any discrimination in violation of this Declaration and against any incitement to such discrimination.

Article 8

Everyone has the right to an effective remedy by the competent national tribunals for acts violating the fundamental rights granted to him by the constitution or by law.

Maulana believed in a non-violent, non-exploitative social and economic order in which justice, social, economic and political shall inform all the institutions of the national life, a system evolved and adopted by the Constituent assembly and now enshrined in our constitution through incorporation of articles covering fundamental rights, directive principles and fundamental duties, that is, Articles 13 to 51A.

Mahatma Gandhi while expressing his views about Maulana Azad, too, had said:

"Maulana Azad is the most forceful, truthful, and fearless *satyagrahi** and fighter against oppression and injustice that I have come across."

Patriotism, Religion, Unity, Culture, History, Literature, Languages and Governance

Maulana Azad was a devout Muslim and a true nationalist and patriot simultaneously and only a person opposed to the

---

* *Satyagraha* is a Sanskrit word meaning non-violent resistance (fighting with peace) started by Mahatma" Gandhi). 'Gandhiji used *satyagraha* in the Indian independence movement and also during his earlier struggle in South Africa. The word '*Satyagrahi*' refers to a non-violent fighter against oppression, injustice and foreign rule.

existence of these two qualities or say, ideologies may express doubt about his credibility.

Jawaharlal Nehru also expressed similar views about him:

"Though I am grateful to all my companions, I would like to mention especially Maulana Abul Kalam Azad, whose erudition has delighted me incredibly, and has sometimes overwhelmed me. In Azad along with the good qualities of the past, the graciousness, the deep learning and tolerance, there is a strange and unique mixture of the urges of today and the modern outlook." "Maulana Azad was a very special representative in a high degree, of the great composite culture which has gradually grown in India. He represented the synthesis of various cultures which had flown in and lost themselves in the ocean of Indian life and humanity, affecting and changing them and being changed themselves by them. In that sense, I can hardly conceive of any other person who can replace him, because the age which produced him is past."

Maulana Azad's Own Views:

"I am a Muslim and profoundly conscious of the fact that I have inherited Islam's glorious tradition of the last fourteen hundred years. I am not prepared to loose even a small part of that legacy. The history and teachings of Islam, its arts and letters, its culture and civilisation are part of my wealth and it is my duty to cherish and guard them……But, with all these feelings, I have another equally deep realisation, born out of my life's experience which is strengthened and not hindered by the Islamic spirit. I am equally proud of the fact that I am an Indian, an essential part of the indivisible unity of the Indian nationhood, a vital factor in its total makeup, without which this noble edifice will remain incomplete."

"If the whole world is our country and is to be honoured, the dust of India has the first place……If all mankind are our brothers, then the Indians have the first place." "Not only is our national freedom impossible without Hindu-Muslim unity, we also cannot create without it, the primary principles of humanity. If an angel were to tell me: "Discard Hindu-Muslim unity and within 24 hours I will give freedom to India"; I would prefer Hindu-Muslim unity. For the delay in the attainment of freedom will be a loss to India alone, but if the Hindu-Muslim unity disappears, that will be a loss to the whole humanity." "It was India's historic destiny that many human races, cultures, and religions should flow to her, and that many a caravan should find rest here......One of the last of these caravans was that of the followers of Islam. This came here and settled for good. In India everything bears the stamp of the joint endeavours of the Hindus and Muslims. Our languages were different, but we grew to use a common language. Our manners and customs were dissimilar, but they produced a new synthesis. No fantasy or artificial scheming to separate and divide us can break this unity."

"In India every kind of faith, every kind of culture, every mode of living was allowed to flourish and find its own salvation."

This is the spirit of Article 27 of the Universal Declaration of Human Rights, too:

Article 27

(1) Everyone has the right freely to participate in the cultural life of the community, to enjoy the arts and to share in scientific advancement and its benefits.

In the December 1912 issue of Al-Hilal, the Maulana wrote:

"For the Hindus, struggle for the independence of the country is a sign of love for the land. But for the Musalmans it is a religious obligation and equivalent to *jihad* in the way of God. And the meaning of *jihad* includes every effort made to establish justice and truth and human rights and the removal of servitude."

During the freedom movement, Maulana always advocated that religion must not be used as an instrument for gaining political power as it is meant for transformation of human soul. He had then declared 'God alone knows what is in the womb of future.'

He had also said:

"Political alliances are based on a spirit of bargaining while cultural contacts deepen mutual understanding."

There is no room for narrow-mindedness in this modern age. We shall find a secular place in the comity of nations only if we are international-minded and tolerant.

He was of the view that history must be based on truth and it should not be subject to distortions. He had suggested:

"We must recast the teaching of history to bring about the unity of men."

"Literary men and women in all the languages can be spurred to greater activity and help in the creation of a literature which is comparable to that of the advanced languages of the world."

Education

His views about education fully commensurate with the provisions contained in Article 26 of the Universal Declaration of Human Rights reproduced below:

Article 26

(1) Everyone has the right to education. Education shall be free, at least in the elementary and fundamental stages. Elementary education shall be compulsory. Technical and professional education shall be made generally available and higher education shall be equally accessible to all on the basis of merit.

(2) Education shall be directed to the full development of the human personality and to the strengthening of respect for human rights and fundamental freedoms. It shall promote understanding, tolerance and friendship among all nations, racial or religious groups, and shall further the activities of the United Nations for the maintenance of peace.

(3) Parents have a prior right to choose the kind of education that shall be given to their children.

Azad's advice given to students several decades ago is relevant even today: To quote:

"Bury communalism once and for all. The student of today is the potential leader of tomorrow. He will have to sustain social, political and economic activities. If he is not properly trained and does not develop the necessary resources of character and knowledge, he cannot supply the leadership which the nation will need."

According to Maulana Azad, the wealth of the nation is not in the country's banks but in primary schools. He had said:

"Every individual has a right to an education that will enable him to develop his facilities and live a full human life. Such education is the birth right of every citizen."

He advocated, in particular, universal primary education, free and compulsory for all children upto the age of 14. Inclusion of Article 21A, though belated one, is the virtual 'documentary replica' of his imaginative concept. University Grants Commission (UGC) was his baby. Now it is a matured legal person. At the same time he patronised institutions teaching and promoting classical languages like Arabic, Persian and Sanskrit. He had also said:

"The nature of education, science and culture is such that their cause can be served better by private and voluntary agencies."

What he had said several decades ago, it has now emerged in its practical form. Now private universities and institutions as also private agencies are playing an important role in serving the cause of education.

He was of the view:

"Science has knit the world in one compact unit, one may say, for the very survival of humanity."

As regards technical education, he strengthened and converted the All India Council for Technical Education into a viable nodal agency for high quality technical education. The Indian Institute of Technology, Kharagpur was established in 1951 followed by IITs at Bombay, Madras, Kanpur and Delhi. The School of Planning and Architecture was also established during his tenure in 1955.

He was also of the view:

"Every student at the secondary level must learn some craft irrespective of the fact whether he or she aims at adopting it as a profession or not."

Our present day skill development programmes are an answer to what Maulana had anticipated more than half a century ago.

He had also predicted and rightly so:

"Indeed, I looked and still look forward to the day when the facilities for technical education in India will be such that people from abroad will come to India for higher scientific and technical education."

The following institutions etc. established during his life time speak of his pragmatic approach and scientific temperament:

1. University Education Commission of 1948
2. Central Advisory Board of Archaeology, 1949

3. Indian Council for Cultural Relations, 1950
4. Delhi Public Library, 1950
5. Indian Institute of Technology, Kharagpur, 1951
6. Secondary Education Commission, 1952
7. National Art Treasures Fund, New Delhi, 1952
8. Central Building Research Institute, Roorkie, 1953
9. Council of Scientific and Industrial Research, 1953
10. National Institute, Pilani, 1953
11. University Grants Commission, 1953
12. National Academy of Letters, New Delhi, 1954
13. Indian Historical Records Commission, Mysore, 1955
14. Reconstitution of All India Council for Technical Education
15. Central Advisory Board of Education, Delhi

He was equally interested in girls' education. He had expressed the following views regarding women education:

Our educational programme will ultimately depend upon the proper education of women, if women take to education, more than half of our problems will be solved. Educated mothers will mean children who can be easily made literate."

He gave new life to and revitalised Anjuman-Tarraqui-e-Urdu-e-Hind and gave reasonable grants to institutions like Jamia Millia Islamia and Aligarh Muslim University to Archaeological Survey of India, an organisation responsible for upkeeping, maintaining and repairing protected historical monuments.

Azad's advice given to students several decades ago, quoted earlier, is relevant even today: To quote:

"Bury communalism once and for all. The student of today is the potential leader of tomorrow. He will have to sustain social, political and economic activities. If he is not properly trained and does not develop the necessary resources of character and knowledge, he cannot supply the leadership which the nation will need."

Maulana Abul Kalam Azad' s views on education fully answer the requirements and spirit of this article. Maulana Abul Kalam Azad has been described by many writers and scribes as an architect of the modern Indian education system, emperor of learning, a person of the caliber of Plato, Aristotle and Pythagoras and above all even those who oppose or opposed him take/took keen interest in his writings.

His views about education and right to education, as detailed above, do not fall short of what is contained in Article 26 of the Universal Declaration of Human Rights. His views are really thought provoking and shall continue to be so for years and years to come.

Maulana Azad stood for a learning society through liberal, modern and universal education with full emphasis on humanism and human values. He was really a store house of knowledge. He was awarded highest award of the country 'Bharat Ratna' for being virtually a Ratna (a word which literally means a jewel, gem, pearl, treasure, anything valuable and desirable, anything excellent or best of its kind).

He firmly believed in composite culture which is generally described as Ganga-Jamni-Tehzeeb (Ganges-Yamuna culture, an euphemism for the mutually participatory co-existence of Hindu and Muslim culture). His following statement quoted earlier, too, bears testimony to it. It was really the voice of his conscience so close to his heart. Though he was a politician but one would never find a disrepute, despicable and defamed word like 'hypocrisy' in his specialised vocabulary. It was an 'out of use' term for him. Whatever he said or wrote he meant that, nothing more, nothing less. To quote:

"If an angel were to descend from the clouds today, settle on the Qutub Minar of Delhi and proclaim from there that India will attain Swaraj provided Hindu-Muslim Unity is renounced, then I would renounce Swaraj and not sacrifice Hindu-Muslim Unity, because if Swaraj is delayed, it is the loss to India, but if Hindu-Muslim Unity is lost, it is the loss to humanity."

CHAPTER 10

Maulana Azad an Exceptionally Honest and Corruption Free Personality

Maulana Azad an honest person of the first order or a corruption free personality, if described in present day terminology, had become a legend in his life time. He led a very simple life. Even a person of ordinary prudene may find it difficult to believe the following report of a Saudi newspaper:

"At the time of his death, he had neither any property nor a bank account. In his personal closet were found some cotton "achkans (long coats buttoned in front)", a dozen "khadi kurtas (shirt like apparel made of thick and coarse kind of cotton cloth)" and pajamas (trousers), two pairs of sandals, an old dressing gown and a used hair brush. But there were lots of rare books which are now the property of the nation."[1]

Maulana Azad like his other freedom fighter companions in the then cabinet was an exceptionally honest man. As a matter of fact most of the leaders in those days who had fought and struggled for the independence of the country were selfless and by and large honest. However, it does not mean that all the present day leaders are corrupt. But at the same time it cannot be denied that absolute honesty is a rare attribute to be found in present day leaders. It is not a situation peculiar to India. It is a disease spread all over the globe. Corruption in a civilised society is a disease like cancer, which if not detected in time is sure to malignise the polity of the country leading to disastrous consequences. It is termed as plague which is not only contagious but if not controlled spreads like fire in a jungle. Its virus is compared with HIV leading to AIDS, being incurable. It has also been termed as a royal thievery. The socio-political system exposed to such a dreaded disease is likely to crumble under its own weight. Corruption is opposed to democracy and social order, being not only anti-people but aimed and targeted against them. It affects the economy and destroys the cultural heritage. Unless nipped in the bud at the earliest, it is likely to cause turbulence shaking the socio-economic political system in an otherwise healthy, wealthy, effective and vibrating society.

There was hardly any substantial specific legislation on the subject at the domestic level or the global one till independence. Only the ordinary penal laws included such provisions. We had no specific law on prevention of corruption till 1947. More legislation followed thereafter in our country.

In Australia, 21 Resiliency Conference, February 2010 it was observed that the conventional view of wealth is money, possessions, and property. But the real wealth of a nation consists of the contributions of its people and nature. So, we need what we haven't had: an economic system that gives visibility and value to the work of caring for people and our Mother Earth.

United Nations Convention against Corruption, 2003

Background

In its resolution 55/61 of 4 December 2000, the General Assembly recognised that an effective international legal instrument against corruption, independent of the United Nations Convention against Transnational Organised Crime (resolution

55/25, annex I) was desirable and decided to establish an ad hoc committee for the negotiation of such an instrument in Vienna at the headquarters of the United Nations Office on Drugs and Crime.

The text of the United Nations Convention against Corruption was negotiated during seven sessions of the Adhoc Committee for the Negotiation of the Convention against Corruption, held between 21 January 2002 and 1 October 2003.

The Convention approved by the Ad Hoc Committee was adopted by the General Assembly by resolution 58/4 of 31 October 2003. The General Assembly, in its resolution 57/169 of 18 December 2002, accepted the offer of the Government of Mexico to host a high-level political Conference for the purpose of signing the convention.

Highlights

Prevention

Corruption can be prosecuted after the fact, but first and foremost, it requires prevention. An entire chapter of the Convention is dedicated to prevention, with measures directed at both the public and private sectors. These include model preventive policies, such as the establishment of anti-corruption bodies and enhanced transparency in the financing of election campaigns and political parties. States must endeavour to ensure that their public services are subject to safeguards that promote efficiency, transparency and recruitment based on merit. Once recruited, public servants should be subject to codes of conduct, requirements for financial and other disclosures, and appropriate disciplinary measures. Transparency and accountability in matters of public finance must also be promoted, and specific requirements are established for the prevention of corruption, in the particularly critical areas of the public sector, such as the judiciary and public procurement. Those who use public services must expect a high standard of conduct from their public servants. Preventing public corruption also requires an effort from all members of society at large. For these reasons, the Convention calls on countries to promote actively the involvement of non-governmental and community-based organisations, as well as other elements of civil society, and to raise public awareness of corruption and what can be done about it. Article 5 of the Convention enjoins each State Party to establish and promote effective practices aimed at the prevention of corruption.

Criminalisation

The Convention requires countries to establish criminal and other offences to cover a wide range of acts of corruption, if these are not already crimes under domestic law. In some cases, States are legally obliged to establish offences; in other cases, in order to take into account differences in domestic law, they are required to consider doing so. The Convention goes beyond previous instruments of this kind, criminalising not only basic forms of corruption such as bribery and the embezzlement of public funds, but also trading in influence and the concealment and laundering of the proceeds of corruption. Offences committed in support of corruption, including money-laundering and obstructing justice, are also dealt with. Convention offences also deal with the problematic areas of private-sector corruption.

International Cooperation

Countries agreed to cooperate with one another in every aspect of the fight against corruption, including prevention, investigation, and the prosecution of offenders. Countries are bound by the Convention to render specific forms of mutual legal assistance in gathering and transferring evidence for use in court, to extradite offenders. Countries are also required to undertake measures which will support the tracing, freezing, seizure and confiscation of the proceeds of corruption.

Asset Recovery

In a major breakthrough, countries agreed on asset-recovery, which is stated explicitly as a fundamental principle of the Convention. This is a particularly important issue for many developing countries where high-level corruption has plundered the national wealth, and where resources are badly needed for reconstruction and the rehabilitation of societies under new governments. Reaching agreement on this chapter has involved intensive negotiations, as the needs of countries seeking the illicit assets had to be reconciled with the legal and procedural safeguards of the countries whose assistance is sought.

Several provisions specify how cooperation and assistance will be rendered. In particular, in the case of embezzlement of public funds, the confiscated property would be returned to the state requesting it; in the case of proceeds of any other offence covered by the Convention, the property would be returned providing the proof of ownership or recognition of the damage caused to a requesting state; in all other cases, priority consideration would be given to the return of confiscated property to the requesting state, to the return of such property to the prior legitimate owners or to compensation of the victims.

Effective asset-recovery provisions will support the efforts of countries to redress the worst effects of corruption while sending at the same time, a message to corrupt officials that there will be no place to hide their illicit assets. Accordingly, Article 51 provides for the return of assets to countries of origin as a fundamental principle of this Convention. Article 43 obliges state parties to extend the widest possible cooperation to each other in the investigation and prosecution of offences defined in the Convention. With regard to asset recovery in particular, the article provides *inter alia* that "In matters of international cooperation, whenever dual criminality is considered a requirement, it shall be deemed fulfilled irrespective of whether the laws of the requested State Party place the offence within the same category of offence or denominate the offence by the same terminology as the requesting State Party, if the conduct underlying the offence for which assistance is sought is a criminal offence under the laws of both States Parties."

Here we may refer to a few stories (based on truth) attributed to Maulana Azad. It was in 1991 when I was working as Assistant Legislative Counsel in Law Ministry my Additional Secretary Shri B.K. Sharma showed me a letter written by Dr Rajendra Prasad, the then President of India, to Maulana Azad recommending a candidate for appointment against a vacant post of translator in official language commission (presently named as official languages wing, Legislative Department, Ministry of Law, Govt. of India). Maulana did not take that letter in good spirit. Rather he felt ill of it and referring to the assurances of freedom fighters of a post-independence transparent administration wrote back to Dr Rajendra Prasad expressing his views in crystal clear language. He, however, appointed the candidate as a translator. It will not be out of place to mention here that the candidate Dr Rajendra Prasad had recommended proved to be a very competent translator. It was a common practice to recommend a right candidate for a right post during those days, particularly by elderly political personalities.

Once during Maulana Azad Memorial Lecture delivered by His Excellency Shri Balmiki Prasad Singh, Governor of Sikkim on 11th November 2011, at Teen Murti Auditorium, New Delhi had narrated the following story:

In June 1948, Prime Minister Nehru chanced upon a large number of paintings of the mother-daughter duo of Hungarian artists, Mrs Sass Brunner and Miss Elizabeth Brunner in Nainital. He purchased a few paintings. On return, he wrote to Maulana Azad recommending eight of their paintings to be acquired by the government at a cost of Rs 15000 (as indicated by the artists).

This matter was sent to the experts, who felt that the price asked for was too high. A series of letters and notes were exchanged. The experts did not yield to the price indicated by the artists. This finally compelled Nehru to observe that if the government was not able to pay the price asked for by the artists, he would pay himself. In a minute dated 23rd September, 1948, Maulana Azad finally closed the matter by saying that 'the bill for the paintings may be sanctioned and the price asked for may be given to the artists'. This kind of sensitivity is worth appreciating and emulating.

Thus, the situation warrants that instead of repenting on our follies, we must strive hard to get rid of corruption. Still we have miles and miles to go! We require many more 'Maulanas' like Maulana Abul Kalam Azad to put our house in order.

Sources :

1. Report published in Saudi Gazette dated Nov. 28, 2014 - Mohammed Saleem Khaleefa, Jeddah.
2. Australia 21 Resiliency Conference, February 2010.
3. United Nations Convention against Corruption, 2003.

Chapter 11

Author's Tribute to A.P.J. Abdul Kalam and His Appreciative Sermons

Some are born great and some are made great but A.P.J. Abdul Kalam (AVUL PAKIR JAINULABDEEN ABDUL KALAM), former President of India, was neither born great nor made great. The term 'made great indicates, though impliedly, as if someone has reached desired heights not of his own but he had been uplifted to reach those heights. If seen from worldly point of view, he was not born great as he was born to the parents who were not well off'. But in the Indian context, it will not be wrong to say that he was born great for two reasons:

1. He was a secular and relegiously neutral person as all of his friends were Hindus. We have desperately been preaching secularism for several decades but he is the man who practiced it at a time when the term did not find mention in any of our statutes. His childhood friends, named below remained dear to him till his death. The following quotation from *"My Childhood,"* an extract taken from the autobiographical book, *'Wings of Fire'* by A.P.J. Abdul Kalam bears testimony to his secular credentials:

   "——*In his childhood he had three close friends- Ramanadha Sastry, Aravindam and Sivaprakashan.*

Once when he was in fifth standard, a new teacher asked him not to sit in the front row along with the high caste Brahmin boys. Abul found Ramanadha Sastry weeping as he went to the last row. This made a lasting impression on Abul. Abul was also greatly influenced by his science teacher, Sivasubramania Iyer. He learnt the lesson of breaking social barriers from him. Iyer invited him to his home for a meal. His wife was an orthodox Brahmin who refused to serve food to a Muslim boy in her so called ritually pure kitchen. Iyer served him with his own hand and sat down beside him to eat his meal. He convinced his wife to serve meal with her own hands and thus was successful in changing the conservative attitude of his wife——."

2. He sought blessings from clergymen professing different religions.

As regards the term 'made great', he was not made great by hook or crook. He was patronised and rightly so for becoming great purely on merit.

We salute him for his simplicity and humility. The attributes or qualities he possessed are hardly found in a single person. He had all qualities of head and heart. Had some other person from such a background reached these heights, he would have developed many negative attributes like pride, obstentation etc. but this gentleman very well knew that pride goeth before a fall. He believed in and practiced 'friendship with all, malice for none'. Has there been any Head of the State in any part of the world who might have entered President House or his official residence with a suit case, a pair of shoes and a few wearing clothes?

Dr Kalam lived and died as a bachelor. All countrymen were the members of his family. He was born for the country and countrymen. Mother earth was as dear to him as his biological mother. For Allama Iqbal, an Urdu poet, 'every particle of Indian soil was *devta* (a deity) for him' was a mere poetic expression but for Kalam it was a physical fact.

Dr Kalam became a father figure in his lifetime. Hats off to him!

A.P.J. Abdul Kalam quotes

"Dream, Dream Dream

Dreams transform into thoughts

And thoughts result in action."

"Dream is not that which you see while sleeping it is something that does not let you sleep."

"Dreams are not those which come while we are sleeping, but dreams are those when we don't sleep before fulfilling them."

"This is my belief: that through difficulties and problems God gives us the opportunity to grow. So when your hopes and dreams and goals are dashed, search among the wreckage, you may find a golden opportunity hidden in the ruins."

Comments

His approach to dreams is pragmatic one. It is not mere day dreaming or fency. For him, it is a vision. Impliedly rather explicitly he is conveying the following message to the people in a poetic language:

"Time is short; art is long; so press on."

"It is very easy to defeat someone, but it is very hard to win someone."

Comments

It is a very positive comment particularly in a society in which intolerance has creeped in or is likely to be crept in. There is no room for hating or maltreating or even humiliating someone in a civilised society. We can pick up a quarrel in a giffy but the reconciliation is always a time consuming process.

"For great men, religion is a way of making friends; small people make religion a fighting tool."

Comments

The quotation conveys the following message:

Friendship with all; malice for none. Dr S. Radhakrishnan former President of India had also said that religion is a dynamic process, a renewed effort of the creative impulses working through exceptional individuals and seeking to uplift humankind to a new level. Maulana Azad had also said that in the domain of religion it appears in the form of blind faith and wants to deceive us in the name of orthodoxy.

As a matter of fact religious harmony and national integration, as contemplated in the Constitution, is the need of the hour but religious fanaticism, which is wrongly described as religious fundamentalism, has plagued the global atmosphere.

The members of different communities get unbalanced by a communal group label, such as, Hindu, Muslim, Sikh or Christian etc. and tend to think irrationally that only members of their own community are always right or just and others are wrong. In that way, they tilt in favour of their own community and discriminate against members of other communities. It is absolutely an irrational approach.

Communal harmony cannot be achieved by fighting or finding fault with each other or criticising each other's religions. It can be achieved only through positive cooperation of all communities and sincere efforts by the State. Good and bad are not to be treated at par. There should be an objective exercise to separate chaff from the grain so that innocent people are not penalised and they are not subject to any inhuman and derogatory treatment and furthermore their human rights that are enshrined in the International covenants and the Constitution of India are not violated.

"Don't take rest after your first victory because if you fail in second, more lips are waiting to say that your first victory was just luck."

"All Birds find shelter during a rain.

But Eagle avoids rain by flying above the Clouds.

"Problems are common, but attitude makes the difference!!!"

"Suffering is the essence of success!!!"

"Be active! Take on responsibility! Work for the things you believe in. If you do not, you are surrendering your fate to others."

"This is my belief: that through difficulties and problems God gives us the opportunity to grow. So when your hopes and dreams and goals are dashed, search among the wreckage, you may find a golden opportunity hidden in the ruins."

- If you fail, never give up because F.A.I.L. means "First Attempt In Learning."

- End is not the end, infact E.N.D. means "Effort Never Dies."

- If you get No as an answer, remember N.O. means "Next Opportunity."

So Let's be positive.

"Man needs difficulties in life because they are necessary to enjoy the success."

"Thinking should become your capital asset, no matter whatever ups and downs you come across in your life."

"Failure will never overtake me if my definition to succeed is strong enough."

"Let not thy winged days be spent in vain. When once gone no gold can buy them back again."

"Desire, when it stems from the heart and spirit, when it is pure and intense, possesses awesome electromagnetic energy. This energy is released into the ether each night, as the mind falls into the sleep state. Each morning it returns to the conscious state reinforced with the cosmic currents. That which has been imaged will surely and certainly be manifested. You can rely, young man, upon this ageless promise as surely as you can rely upon the eternally unbroken promise of sunrise...and of Spring."

"Why be afraid of difficulties, sufferings and problems? When troubles come, try to understand the relevance of your sufferings. Adversity always presents opportunities for introspection."

"Once your mind stretches to a new level it never goes back to its original dimension."

Comments

All these quotes are quite inspiring and indicate APJ's dynamism. It is an advice to the youngmen to be optimistic and come out of vicious circle(s) in compelling situations(s).This positive attitude can take them to any heights.

"Learning gives creativity

Creativity leads to thinking

Thinking provides knowledge

Knowledge makes you great."

"Thinking is the capital, Enterprise is the way, Hard Work is the solution."

"When learning is purposeful, creativity blossoms. When creativity blossoms, thinking emanates. When thinking emanates, knowledge is fully lit. When knowledge is lit, economy flourishes."

Comments

All these three quotes are also equally inspiring and indicate APJ's dynamism and indomitable Spirit. It is the corroboration of Maulana Azad's view expressed in the All India Educational Conference held in January,1948. To quote:

"Do not forget that you can seal all your worldly possessions with national and geographical limits but no seal can be put on learning and civilisation——In learning and culture it makes an appeal to us in the name of our nation and country."

"Your children are not your children. They are the sons and daughters of Life's longing for itself. They come through you but not from you. You may give them your love but not your thoughts. For they have their own thoughts."

"Behind the parents stands the school, and behind the teacher the home."

"Sometimes, it's better to bunk a class and enjoy with friends, because now, when I look back, marks never make me laugh, but memories do."

"We are all born with a divine fire in us. Our efforts should be to give wings to this fire and fill the world with the glow of its goodness."

Comments

Blending of humour, satire and an advice to be read between the lines.

"The sides of the mountain sustain life, not the peak. This is where things grow, experience is gained, and technologies are mastered. The importance of the peak lies only in the fact that it defines the sides."

Comments

He perhaps means to say that Rome was not built in a day. One has to find a way or make one. One cannot reach desired heights in one go. One has to learn the art, attain technical knowledge and find out the areas where one can make best use of one's talents.

"What makes life in Indian organisations difficult is the widespread prevalence of this very contemptuous pride. It stops us from listening to our juniors, subordinates and people down the line. You cannot expect a person to deliver results if you humiliate him, nor can you expect him to be creative if you abuse him or despise him. The line between firmness and harshness, between strong leadership and bullying, between discipline and vindictiveness is very fine, but it has to be drawn."

Comments

Let our bureaucrats ponder over it and ensure follow up action. It is not a mere sermon; it is the basic requirement for smooth administration.

Sources

Ignited Minds: Unleashing the Power Within India by A.P.J. Abdul Kalam.

Turning Points: A Journey Through Challenges.

India 2020: A Vision For The New Millennium by A.P.J. Abdul Kalam.

*My Journey: Transforming Dreams into Actions*by A.P.J. Abdul Kalam.

Target 3 Billion: Innovative Solutions Towards Sustainable Development by A.P.J. Abdul Kalam, Srijan Pal Singh.

Indomitable Spirit by A.P.J. Abdul Kalam.

Inspiring Thoughts by A.P.J. Abdul Kalam.

The Scientific Indian: A Twenty-first Century Guide to the World around Us by A.P.J. Abdul Kalam, Y.S. Rajan.

Mission India: A Vision for Indian Youth by A.P.J. Abdul Kalam.

You Are Born To Blossom: Take My Journey Beyond. by A.P.J. Abdul Kalam, Arun K. Tiwari.

You are Unique: Scale New Heights by Thoughts and Actions by A.P.J. Abdul Kalam, Poonam S. Kohli (Editor), Neha Gouse (Illustrator).

Forge your Future by A.P.J. Abdul Kalam.

The Life Tree, Poems by A.P.J. Abdul Kalam.

Envisioning an Empowered Nation: Technology for Societal Transformation by A.P.J. Abdul Kalam.

Governance for Growth in India by A.P.J. Abdul Kalam.

Guiding Souls by A.P.J. Abdul Kalam, Arun Tiwari.

The Luminous Sparks by A.P.J. Abdul Kalam.

Spirit of India by A.P.J. Abdul Kalam.

Reignited: Scientific Pathways to a Brighter Future by A.P.J. Abdul Kalam.

Beyond 2020: A Vision for Tomorrow's India by A.P.J. Abdul Kalam, Y.S. Rajan.

India My Dream by A.P.J. Abdul Kalam.

A Manifesto for Change: A Sequel to INDIA 2020 by A.P.J. Abdul Kalam, V Ponraj.

Transcendence My Spiritual Experiences with Pramukh Swamiji by A.P.J. Abdul Kalam.

Thoughts for Change: We Can Do it by A.P.J. Abdul Kalam, A. Pillai Sivathanu.

Evolution of Enlightened Societies by A.P.J. Abdul Kalam.

Ignited Minds by A.P.J. Abdul Kalam.

Squaring the Circle:Seven Steps to Indian Renaissance by A.P.J. Abdul Kalam.

Children Ask Kalam by A.P.J. Abdul Kalam.

Scientist To President by A.P.J. Abdul Kalam.

The Guiding Light: A Selection of Quotations from My Favourite Books by A.P.J. Abdul Kalam.

Chapter 12

Biography of A.P.J. Abdul Kalam (1931-2015)

A.P.J. Abdul Kalam (Avul Pakir Jainulabdeen Abul Kalam), former President of India, a great scientist, popularly known as missile man, recognised and loved as a national hero for his valuable contribution in the field of space research, was born to Jainulabdeen (to be correctly spelled as Zainulabedeen) and Ashiamma on October 15, 1931 in Rameshwaram, Tamil Nadu (then being a part of Madras, a presidency town during British rule). He did not come from a well off family but he was born with a prospective silver spoon in his mouth and as such he did many odd jobs (including that of a newspaper hawker) to support the family (his parents etc.) and afford his educational expenses. He never gave up on his education for want of money or some other constraints. He graduated from Saint Joseph's College, Tiruchirappalli in 1954 and then proceeded to Madras later next year to study aerospace engineering at the Madras Institute of Technology (MIT).

Academic and Professional Career

After graduating from Madras Institute of Technology (MIT), Kalam joined as chief scientist in Defence Research and Development Organisation (DRDO) but he soon shifted to the

Indian Space Research Organisation (ISRO) probably for a better career and worked as project director of India's first indigenous Satellite Launch Vehicle there. His years at the ISRO transformed him into the icon of the Indian space research mission.Thereafter, Kalam directed two projects, namely, Project Devil and Project Valiant in seventees.These projects were taken upto develop ballistic missiles from the technology of the successful SLV programme. Launching of Rohini-1 into the space, using the SLV rocket, was a great achievement of Indian scientists. After successful launching of Rohini-1 into the space, the government decided to take up advanced missile programme and this job was also entrusted to Kalam, being its director. The nation shall even remain indebted to him for his valuable contribution in developing missiles under the missions "Agni and Prithvi." India owes its emergence as a nuclear nation to Kalam's organisational and technical support for Pokhran-II nuclear tests in 1998, the first such tests after a gap of 24 years. He was the Chief Executive of the Integrated Guided Missile Development Programme (I.G.M.D.P), too.

While recognising valuable services of Dr Kalam rendered to the country, he was appointed as the Chief Scientific Adviser to the Prime Minister and the Secretary of Defence Research and Development Organisation. It will not be out of place to mention here that many an Indian Administrative Service (IAS) Officer cannot reach these heights, that is getting the rank of secretary to Government of India, even at the fag end of their career. Kalam held this office for long seven years from 1992 to 1999. It was during the tenure of this office that Kalam served as the Chief Project Coordinator for Pokhran II nuclear tests, after which he was popularly and rightly called the "Missile Man of India", a title sufficient to perpetuate his memory for all times to come. Kalam succeeded K. R. Narayan to serve as the 11th President of India from 2002 until 2007 with the support of all major political parties of India. However, second term eluded him.

His Legacy

APJ Abdul Kalam has not left behind any wealth or property worth mentioning; he has left behind just a legacy of hope, optimism, positivism, self-confidence, determination and above all 20-20 vision and the books written by him, degrees of Doctor of Science (D.Sc. Honoris-causa) conferred by various universities and the following awards he received during his life time:

Bharat Ratna (1997)

Padma Vibhushan (1990)

Padma Bhushan (1981)

Indira Gandhi Award for National Integration (1997)

Veer Savarkar Award (1998)

Ramanujan Award (2000)

King Charles II Medal (2007)

International von Kármán Wings Award (2009)

Hoover Medal (2009)

National Design Award

Dr Biren Roy Space Award

Professor Y Nayudamma Memorial Gold Medal (1996)

GM Modi Award for Science (1996)

R K Firodia Award for Excellence in S&T (1996)

(The list is indicative only)

Dr Kalam received laurels from all the institutions represented through eminent personalities during conferment of honorary degrees for his contribution to science and technology. A press release by Scotland's prestigious University of Edinburgh in 2014 conferring degree of Doctor of Science (D.Sc. Honoris-causa) on Dr Kalam is the virtual replica of all earlier pre-conferment addresses. The university release contained following words of appreciation for Dr Kalam:

"The award – presented by University Principal and Vice Chancellor Timothy O'Shea – is in recognition of Dr Kalam's outstanding contribution to science and technology, and his commitment to helping transform India into a developed nation by 2020," the varsity said today. Kalam, who served as the President of India from 2002 to 2007, received the degree during a dinner held in his honour on May 15. The 82-year-old, who is regarded as the father of India's missile programme, has in recent years campaigned to highlight the plight of India's rural poor, advocating the use of technology to address social and economic inequalities.

O'Shea also said: "It is a privilege to welcome Dr Kalam to Edinburgh and to present him with an honorary degree." It (the university) recognises his extraordinary work as a scientist, as a figurehead for his country and for working to tackle rural poverty and injustice over many years."

The press release issued by Press Information Bureau on Monday August 3, 2015 is the most authentic version of APJ Abdul Kalam's life, achievements and above all his mindset:

"AVUL PAKIR JAINULABDEEN ABDUL KALAM

Born on 15th October, 1931 at Rameshwaram in Tamil Nadu, Bharat Ratna Avul Pakir Jainulabdeen Abul Kalam assumes the office of the President of the Republic of India on July 25, 2002.

From a humble beginning, Dr Kalam had an unparalleled career as an Aerospace and Defence Scientist, leading the nation with a vision of "Developed India." Dr Kalam as an eminent Aeronautical Engineer, contributed for the development of India's first Satellite Launch Vehicle, SLV III, became the architect of Indian Guided Missile development programme, led to the successful Nuclear experiments and envisioned a road map for realising "Developed India" within 20 years.

A graduate from the St. Joseph's College, Tiruchirapalli, Abul Kalam later studied aeronautical engineering in the Madras Institute of Technology which was regarded as the crown jewel of technical education in Southern India in the fifties. After passing out as a graduate aeronautical engineer, Abul Kalam joined the Directorate of Technical Development and Production of the Ministry of Defence.

He later joined the Indian Committee for Space Research (INCOSPAR) as a Rocket Engineer, which during the later half of 1962 had decided to set up the Equatorial Rocket Launching Station at Thumba. He became a member of team led by Professor Vikram Sarabai which aimed at organising an integrated national space programme for the manufacture of rockets and launch vehicles indigenously.

Dr Abul Kalam was chosen to lead a team for the design and development of Satellite Launch Vehicle, SLV III which was successfully launched on 18th July, 1980, injecting Rohini satellite into low earth orbit. He later became Director of ISRO Launch Vehicles/Systems and contributed for the evolution of launch vehicle configurations.

Dr Abul Kalam was appointed Director of the Defence Research and Development Laboratory, Hyderabad in 1982. As Director, DRDL, he was the Chief of Integrated Guided Missile Development Programme and led to successful completion of Prithvi and Agni missiles. He was appointed as the Scientific Advisor to the Defence Minister, Secretary to Department of Defence Research and Development and Director General of Defence Research and Development Organisation in 1992.

Many new technology projects towards building self-reliance in defence and also spin-off to society emerged during this period. Later he became the Principal Scientific Advisor to the Government of India in the rank of Cabinet Minister and served in this capacity from November 1999 till November 2001. He was primarily responsible for evolving policies, strategies and missions for generation of innovations in technology development for multiple applications through government departments, academic institutions and industries as partners. Dr Kalam was also the Chairman, Ex-officio of the Scientific Advisory Committee to the Cabinet (SAC-C). Dr Kalam believes that Technology can be used as a tool for national development. In December 2001, he moved over to Anna University as Professor of Technology and Societal Transformation.

Dr APJ Abdul Kalam has been awarded Padma Bhushan in 1981, Padma Vibhushan in 1990 and Bharat Ratna in 1997.

Dr Kalam was conferred with the degree of Doctor of Science (Dr Sc. Honoris-causa) by twenty eight universities. He is the recipient of several awards including the National Design Award; Dr Biren Roy Space Award; Prof. Y Nayudamma Memorial Gold Medal (1996); GM Modi Award for Science (1996); R K Firodia Award for Excellence in S&T (1996); Veer Savarkar Award (1998) and Indira Gandhi Award for National Integration (1997).

He is a Fellow of many professional societies including Aeronautical Society of India; Astronautical Society ; Indian National Academy of Engineering ; Indian Academy of Sciences and Institution of Electronics and Telecommunication Engineers.

Dr Kalam is a connoisseur of classical Carnatic music. He plays veena in his leisure. He writes poetry in Tamil, his mother tongue.

Seventeen of his poems were translated into English and published in 1994 as a book entitled "*My Journey*." He is also the Author of three books in English – "*India 2020 : A vision for the New Millennium*", "*Wings of Fire : an Autobiography*" and "*Ignited Minds – unleashing the power within India.*"

PIB Release regarding Cabinet condolence on the death of former President Dr A P J Abul Kalam

The Union Cabinet has expressed profound sorrow at the sad demise of former President of India, Dr A.P.J. Abdul Kalam. In a resolution passed at a special Cabinet Meeting this morning, it said, "in his passing away the country has lost a visionary scientist, a true nationalist and a great son." The Cabinet met under the Chairmanship of Prime Minister, Shri Narendra Modi and extended its heart-felt condolences to the bereaved family on behalf of the Government and the entire nation. The former President breathed his last at Bethany Hospital, Shillong, Meghalaya on 27th July, 2015.

The following is the text of the Resolution:

"Born on 15th October, 1931 at Rameswaram in Tamil Nadu, Dr Avul Pakir Jainulabdeen Abul Kalam, specialised in Aeronautical Engineering from Madras Institute of Technology. Dr Kalam made significant contribution in developing India's first indigenous Satellite Launch Vehicle and made India an exclusive member of Space Club. Popularly known as the "Missile Man of India", Dr Kalam was responsible for the development and operationalisation of AGNI and PRITHVI Missiles. He gave thrust to self-reliance in defence systems by introducing Light Combat Aircraft. Dr Kalam was the Scientific Adviser to Defence Minister and Secretary, Department of Defence Research and Development during 1992-99. During this period, strategic missile systems were developed and the Pokhran-II nuclear tests were conducted. Dr Kalam had served as the Principal Scientific Advisor to the Government of India, from 1999 to 2001 and was responsible for evolving policies, strategies and missions for many development applications and piloted India Millennium Mission 2020. In his literary pursuit, Dr Kalam's books - "Wings of Fire", "India 2020 -A Vision for the New Millennium", "My journey" and "Ignited Minds - Unleashing the power within India" became household names in India and abroad. Dr Kalam was passionate about transforming society through technology, in particular by inspiring the youth of India to harness science and technology for human welfare. Dr Kalam was the recipient of many national and international awards including honorary doctorates from 48 Universities from India and abroad. He received the country's highest civilian Award "Bharat Ratna" in the year 1997. Eventually, from a very humble beginning, he rose to the highest office of the Country and served as the 11th President of India from 2002 to 2007. During his tenure, he was affectionately known as the People's President."

CHAPTER 13

Maulana Abul Kalam Azad and APJ Abdul Kalam-A Note of Commendation

Maulana Abul Kalam Azad was born in an orthodox religious family. He had to get rid of his legacy (orthodoxy all around) and demolish the old structure to raise the new one. He was imparted religious education to become a *Maulvi* (a clergyman in holy Islamic order) who may become an Imam (one who leads the prayer) or Mufti (a juriconsult who notifies the decisions of the Muslim Law, in or representing, cases submitted to him or an expounder of Muslim Law) subsequently. He was taught Arabic and Persian first to get himself acquainted with Muslim Theology and Jurisprudence and then Philosophy, Geometry, Mathematics and Algebra. It was through self-study that he also learnt English, and acquired knowledge of world history, and political science so that he may keep pace with the changing world and acquire latest knowledge about modern world and changing global socio-political scenario. On the other hand, APJ Abdul Kalam received by and large modern education right from his childhood in a non-communal atmosphere. He was a secular and religiously neutral person as all of his friends were Hindus. It, however, does not mean that a person having friends from his own community should be called communal. It was just a feather in Kalam's cap. He is the man who practiced secularism at a time when the term did not find mention in any of our statutes. His childhood Hindu friends remained dear to him till his death. He also sought blessings from clergymen professing different religions. Thus, he remained a part of the national mainstream from day one but Maulana had to face stiff opposition from his own community. It was not so easy for him to come out of this vicious circle but he did. Even after partition communal strife did not shake his conviction. He continued to tell Indian Muslims that now Indian politics has taken a new direction and the moot question before Indian Muslims now is whether or not they are capable of constructive thinking. He further said 'the gloom cast upon your lives is momentary; I assure you we can be beaten by none save our own selves! I have always said, and I repeat it again today; eschew your indecisiveness, your mistrust, and stop your misdeeds. This unique triple-edged weapon is more lethal than the two-edged iron sword which inflicts fatal wounds, which I have heard of !"

Those who have short memory and a particular bent of mind blame that nationalist Muslims like Abul Kalam Azad and the then Jamiat Ulema-e-Hind president Maulana Hussain Ahmad Madani opposed Pakistan only because they felt that Partition would affect Muslim domination in the sub-continent and Muslims would heavily lose or to extract a heavy price from the Congress for their patriotism in the name of minority protection. They also say that Azad's agreeing to a proposal of rotating Indian headship which meant that India would have a Hindu and then a Muslim head of State and army chief by turns, reflected his subjectivity. As a matter of fact it does not reflect his subjectivity. Fact of the matter is that it reflects their subjectivity and stereotype outlook. Had this fire brand leader been on the other side, history of India's independence would have been different and many the then Muslim leaders would not have come into lime light. Indian history can never ignore this great man even with the change of guard or change in the system of governance.

Maulana Azad shall always be remembered for his political achievements and the sacrifices he made for the country in a very difficult and extremely adverse situation and stiff opposition from his own community (pre-partition Muslims) whereas APJ Abdul Kalam would be remembered for his technical contribution to the country and as a symbol and practical example of India really being a secular country –a country in which son of a Muslim fisherman can get an opportunity to receive best education and become head of state of the biggest democracy of the world.

Let the nation salute both of them for centuries and centuries to come.

Hazaron saal Nargis apni benoori pe roti hai
bari mushkil se hota(e) hai(n) chaman mein didawar paida

For a thousand years the Narcissus has been lamenting its blindness; With great difficulty the one(s) with true vision is (are) born.

Index